Runaway World

ANTHONY GIDDENS

RUNAWAY WORLD

How Globalisation is Reshaping our Lives

Routledge
Taylor & Francis Group
New York London

Routledge
Taylor and Francis Group
270 Madison Avenue
New York, NY 10016

Routledge
Taylor and Francis Group
2 Park Square
Milton Park, Abingdon
Oxon OX14 4RN

Library of Congress Cataloging-in-Publication Data

Giddens, Anthony.
    Runaway world : how globalization is reshaping our lives/
    Anthony Giddens.
    p.cm.
    Includes bibliographical references and index.
    ISBN 0-415-92719-6 (hb)—0-415-94487-2 (pb)

To Michele and Katy

Contents

Preface to the
second edition

I gave the BBC talks on which this book is based
more than three years ago. The theme of the book
– the transformative impact of globalisation upon
our lives – has become even more widely debated now
than it was then. The term 'globalisation' has itself
become ever more globalised. There can be few quasi-
technical words that have achieved such wide currency.

When I was writing the talks, in late 1998, the anti-
globalisation movement had barely got going. Since that
date, many thousands of demonstrators opposing globalisation have taken to the streets, in cities ranging from
Seattle to Buenos Aires, Gothenburg and Genoa. Moreover, no one three years ago anticipated the events of
11 September 2001.

Each of these sets of developments demands analysis,
but I should say at the outset that there is little or
nothing in the text of the book which I would want
to change in the light of them. Consider first what

happened on 11 September. All the sections of the book are relevant to the events of that day and their aftermath. Intensifying globalisation, documented in the opening chapter, furnishes both the context of the attacks and the means that made them possible. The terrorists' target was the United States, the prime global power. They used jet aircraft as destructive weapons. In staging the events as they did, they had in mind a global media audience. The second plane crashed into the South Tower of the World Trade Centre about half an hour after the first – guaranteeing dramatic television coverage. It has been estimated that a billion people across the world saw the second plane hit the South Tower in real time.

The concern of the second chapter, risk, speaks for itself. The events of 11 September 2001 have alerted us to risks about which most people previously – including states' leaders – were quite sanguine. Whatever happens to Al-Qaeda, the destruction of the Trade Towers and the damaging of the Pentagon will almost certainly not be the only examples of major terrorist activity organised on a transnational basis. We have become newly conscious of the vulnerabilities that can be exploited by terrorist action, such as the targeting of nuclear power plants, the poisoning of water supplies, or the propagation of deadly diseases.

The titles of the other three chapters – tradition, family and democracy – might seem more remote, but they are not. Al-Qaeda is a fundamentalist movement.

There is an intimate and inseparable relation between tradition and fundamentalism, as I try to make clear. Fundamentalist ideas are by no means limited to Islam, or indeed to religion more generally. Fundamentalist groups and struggles can come into being in any sphere where traditional beliefs and practices are becoming corroded.· Fundamentalism – religious, nationalist or ethnic – is always edged with the possibility of violence, since it is the antithesis of tolerance. To the fundamentalist, there is only one right and proper way of life, and everyone else had better get out of the way.

A preoccupation with the family, and particularly with the changing role of women, is in turn at the core of some of the major forms of fundamentalism, particularly those of a religious variety. Religious fundamentalists want to roll back modernity – and nowhere more obviously so than in respect of the emancipation of women. Whether in the shape of the American religious right, or Islamic movements, the fundamentalists are vociferous defenders of the traditional family, and hostile to the attempts of women to break away from their traditional social and cultural roles. And of course they are also commonly antagonistic to democracy, the very principles of which depend upon universal rights.

Nations today, I say in the original text, mostly no longer have enemies, but instead face risks and dangers. Have the events of 11 September 2001 rendered this statement inappropriate or false? I don't think so.

Intensifying globalisation has radically altered the nature of nation-states, and their modes of relating to each other, especially the industrial nations. A large number of nations have given up the impulse to invade or conquer one another. Belligerent states still exist in various parts of the world, such as Iraq under Saddam Hussein. But the most important sources of danger, for industrial and developing countries alike, lie in failed or collapsing states, together with the fears and hatreds such situations engender. Afghanistan is an obvious example. Countries struggling against poverty, bearing the long-term impact of colonialism and the Cold War, or both, and where government lacks legitimacy, are breeding grounds for resentment and despair. They can become havens for transnational networks, which, as the rise of Al-Qaeda showed, can provide a very real source of threat to the integrity of nations.

The events of 11 September 2001 prompted a flurry of speculative writing. Did they form a watershed in current world history? Is it true, as was so commonly said at the time, that 'the world will never be the same again'? The easiest way to consider these questions is to consider the world on 10 September 2001. How different would the world situation look today if the terrorist attacks in the United States had either failed or not taken place?

It is clear that 11 September was less of a fault-line in history than many commentators, reeling from the unexpected and impossible nature of what happened, asserted at the time. The opening of the Berlin Wall in 1989 was a far more signal event for contemporary history than the attacks on New York and Washington – indeed, in some respects it was the backdrop to them. The militant Islamic groups that created Al-Qaeda, after all, originally were actively supported by the Americans during the latter phases of the Cold War, as a means of ejecting the Soviets from Afghanistan. With the ending of the Cold War, neither the West nor Russia took much further interest in what happened in Afghanistan, leaving the country to stew in the mess they had helped to create. Much the same happened in other parts of the globe, including other regions in Asia, Africa and Central and Southern Africa. Many of the failing states of the world are located in areas where the two super-powers during the Cold War period fought their battles by proxy.

The events of 11 September 2001 may have changed the world less than many have claimed, but the initial responses to them were not all over-exaggerated. Prior to that day no heartlands area in a Western state had been attacked by a non-Western force for over three centuries. The only other example, the Japanese bombing of Pearl Harbor, occurred in a relatively isolated outpost. Terrorist groups of various kinds have steadily been building up transnational networks – the IRA, for example, has connections with a range of other insurgent organisations, and has received support from within the United States, and from Libya, Cuba and Iran, among other countries. But most terrorist acts previously have killed and injured quite small numbers of people. Less than 1,500 people died, for instance, over thirty years of the troubles in North Ireland as a result of terrorist violence. The attacks of 11 September not only killed some 4,000, they were aimed at the nerve centres of American power – probably including the White House as well as the buildings that were actually hit. The cost of them to the US economy has been put at $640 billion.

The campaign of the United States and its allies in Afghanistan may have severely damaged Al-Qaeda, but much of the organisation's network remains intact. Whether or not Al-Qaeda itself carries out further attacks, the mode in which it was set up may well serve as a model for others in the future. It has or had a membership structure operative in the United States, several of the major countries of Europe and the Middle East as well as Asia. The sophistication, planning and coordination involved in the 11 September attacks were of a level normally associated with a state rather than a dissident group. Before the current global era it is impossible to imagine that comparable events could have occurred, reflecting as they do our new-found interdependence. The rise of global terrorism, like world-wide networks involved in money-laundering, drug-running and other forms of organised crime, are all parts of the dark side of globalisation.

The events of 11 September 2001 therefore do mark a significant development in patterns of confrontation and violence in the current world order, the full consequences of which we can only guess at. There have also already been geopolitical shifts of some significance. The United States and Russia, for instance, have drawn closer together in the face of what their leaderships see as shared threats. The Russians have softened their opposition to the plans of the United States to construct a system of missile defence.

It would seem obvious that world-wide terrorist networks can only be combated through world-wide collaboration, both among nations, and between nations and other agencies. The sharing of information, cooperation in the gathering of intelligence, and mutual planning to reduce strategic vulnerabilities, would seem the ways forward. So far, however, little of this has been forthcoming. The Bush administration in the United States came into power determined to follow a more unilateralist line than the outgoing president, Bill Clinton, had pursued. President Bush refused to sign up to the Kyoto accord on climate change, rejected the attempts of OECD to regulate tax havens and has disavowed the treaty designed to counter chemical warfare. Some of these earlier positions were modified after 11 September, but the thrust of America's position has remained the same. The Bush administration does not accept the need for an International Court of Criminal

Law, and seeks to weaken the strength of international law rather than bolster it. The budget of the military has been upped considerably, in spite of the fact that the United States is already stronger militarily than all the other industrial nations put together. The object of the American military planners is quite clear and explicit: the United States is to be capable of winning any armed conflict in which it might become engaged, anywhere on earth, as well as in outer space.

President Bush has described 11 September 2001 and its aftermath as 'a new kind of war'. But his response thus far is more attuned to traditional forms of warfare and national security than to the challenge of the global age. Security can no longer be wholly or even primarily national, even for the most powerful state in the world. Military preparedness is essential, but even the most sophisticated weaponry can be outflanked, or can simply be irrelevant to combating organisations whose aims and methods have nothing to do with conquering territory. 'Global guerrillas' will be just as difficult to defeat militarily as guerrillas have proved to be on more local terrain. Guerrilla wars almost always have only been brought to an end through political means – through compromise, negotiation and dealing with the problems that sparked off insurgency in the first place. The same applies on a global level.

The attacks on the World Trade Centre and the Pentagon were by no means condemned across the world.

Many with grievances against the United States, and against the West as a whole, saw them as a justified strike against an oppressor. Anti-Americanism is a common sentiment, not only in Arab and Islamic nations or communities, but in a diversity of other nations besides. Some forms of hatred towards the United States and the West are based upon a mixture of regional and religious antagonisms, especially in the Middle East. Hostility towards Israel, and to the United States as its main patron, has become the driving force of political life and culture in most Arab states, and has fuelled the rise of brutal regimes in Iraq and Syria. In the era of instantaneous communications, it has become a key component of Islamic fundamentalism world-wide. No 'war against terrorism' will get very far unless there is a concerted effort made – and one that would involve the UN and the wider world community – to achieve a resolution of the Israel-Palestine issue.

Anti-Americanism and anti-Western feeling are also widespread in societies that are not Islamic, and where the conflicts of the Middle East are not an issue – in particular in the poorer parts of the world. Western policy is seen as the source of poverty and under-development. These beliefs often have a foundation in fact. The parlous condition of some African countries, for example, reflects the long-term impact of Western colonialism and the more recent involvements of Western powers during the Cold War period. But they have often today become generalised to globalisation itself. Globalisation is widely seen in the developing world as merely the latest stage in the exploitation of the third world by the West – a project from which the rich countries gain at the expense of the poor.

Nor are such beliefs confined to those living in poor countries. They are shared by many in the anti-globalisation movement, whose activities have grown apace since the World Trade Organisation meetings in Seattle on 30 November 1999. Since then, mass protests organised by the anti-globalisers have taken place in many cities. For a few months after 11 September 2001, the anti-globalisation movement seemed to become disorientated and fragmented. During the early phases of the American action in Afghanistan, some groups involved with the movement broke away to protest against the US incursion, believing it to be both unjustified and likely to produce a humanitarian disaster in the country. However, the movement has now regrouped and has again begun to stage mass street demonstrations.

What do the demonstrators want? What does it mean to be 'anti-globalisation'? A diversity of different groups have in fact been involved in the demonstrations, having varying aims and ambitions. Some, a small minority, have connections to anarchism. Others declare themselves to be not just against globalisation but 'anti-capitalism'. A few are prepared to use violence to further their ends. The vast majority, however, are concerned with peaceful protest.

Three themes repeatedly surface, even among those whose views might differ in other ways. One, as I mention in Chapter I, harks back to anti-Americanism and jaundiced views about the West. Globalisation, it is held, essentially advances the interests of the United States and the other Western countries. It is more or less identical to Americanisation – hence the favourite targets of some of the demonstrators, McDonald's, Starbucks, or shops selling Nike goods.

The second concerns the role of the big corporations, of whom these names are representative. The largest companies in the world, those in the anti-globalisation movement point out, have an annual turnover higher than the GDP of all but a few nations. They have usurped some of the power that should belong to sovereign democratic states. They are able to roam the world looking for the cheapest sources of raw materials and labour, and are able to ride roughshod over the interests of poorer countries in so doing.

However, the really important issue to many in the anti-globalisation movement is world inequality. The inequalities between rich and poor, they believe, are growing, and globalisation is the prime force responsible. Here we come back to 11 September 2001, since the widening gulf between the affluent few and the impoverished majority, it is said, creates the feelings of resentment and despair that helped prompt the attacks.

Is globalisation geared to the concerns of America and the other rich nations? There is plainly a good deal of truth in the assertion. The United States is easily the dominant power in the world, militarily, economically and culturally. Most of the world's biggest companies are American, and all the top fifty corporations have their home base in one or other of the industrial countries. The vast majority of internet users are in the rich societies. The wealthier countries dominate some of the most influential world agencies, such as G8, the World Bank and the IMF – and also, many would say, the UN. World society is radically imbalanced in respect of who holds the levers of power and who does not.

Yet globalisation today is not a simple recapitulation of the past, and it is not identical either with Americanisation or Westernisation. The dominance of the United States, and the West more generally, over the rest of the world could be said to operate on three levels – the economic, the geopolitical and the cultural. The United States is easily the largest economy in the world and, whether one likes it or not, is the main motor of the global economy as a whole. The prosperity or otherwise of the American economy at any one point in time affects the progress of virtually every other economy in the world. But neither the United States, nor the industrial countries as a whole, control the global economy, which is far too complex and encompassing for any nation or groups of nations to bend to their own will.

Geopolitically, the United States is now the world's only super-power, but its overall influence is probably less than it was during the Cold War period. During that time, America was able to intervene in large parts of the world, building up a gigantic series of coalitions directed towards containing the spread of communism. Today, its global influence is more diffuse. In spite of President Bush's apparent turn towards unilateralism, there is little the United States can do in most contexts without the collaboration of other nations. Geopolitically, the world is becoming more polycentric. The EU has nothing like the military muscle of the United States, but nevertheless is becoming more and more of an independent player in world affairs. Russia retains its potential as a major power. Japan, South Korea and China continue to develop their geopolitical clout, and India is certain to assume a more powerful influence in world affairs than it has had hitherto. These changes are already affecting the composition of world bodies, where there is much more direct involvement of non-Western countries than there used to be – a trend that needs to be promoted further.

American involvement is of course of crucial importance in the reform of global institutions and agreements. But if such involvement is not forthcoming, the rest of the world can often push on anyway. The Kyoto agreements have been endorsed by 53 nations, in spite of the refusal of the United States to sign up. As of April 2002, 66 countries had ratified the treaty to establish the International Criminal Court. America has opposed the idea of the court since 139 other nations first approved it in 1998, at a meeting in Rome under the auspices of the UN. The United States maintains its hostility to the proposals, but the court will come into existence, and will provide the means of putting on trial political leaders accused of crimes of genocide or mass murder.

Western, and more specifically American, cultural influence is visible everywhere – in films, television, popular music and other areas. Cultural standardisation is an intrinsic part of this process. Yet all this is a relatively superficial cultural veneer; a more profound effect of globalisation is to produce greater local cultural diversity, not homogeneity. The United States itself is the very opposite of a cultural monolith, comprising as it does a dazzling variety of different ethnic and cultural groups. Because of its 'push down' effect, discussed in the text, globalisation tends to promote a renewal of local cultural identities. Sometimes these reflect wider world patterns, but very often they self-consciously diverge from them.

We need a similarly nuanced view of the role of the big corporations. Those who are critical of the expansion of corporate power have important points to make. Corporations can threaten the democratic legitimacy of states, in the industrial as well as the developing countries, where they are able to buy votes or dominate the funding of political parties. Some corporations act irresponsibly in their dealings across the world. For instance, they may manipulate their operations so as to minimise the tax they pay in their parent country, or avoid paying taxes altogether. They may be indifferent to the social and environmental consequences that their policies or products have.

Yet the power of the big companies can easily be exaggerated – and is greatly exaggerated by those who say that corporations 'run the world'. Nations, especially where they act collaboratively, have far more power than corporations, and will continue to do so for the indefinite future. Nations have control of territory, corporations do not; nations establish frameworks of law, corporations do not; nations control military power, corporations do not. As globalisation advances, it actually becomes more difficult for the big companies to act irresponsibly, rather than the other way round. A major reason is the rise of NGOs (non-governmental organisations) – which have the capability to monitor what companies do, in any part of the world, and to bring sanctions to bear upon them. Organisations like Greenpeace or Oxfam are themselves global in scope. They can have a very significant impact upon what corporations do by bringing corporate malpractices to public attention, and mobilising opposition to them. In some respects the larger a corporation is, the more vulnerable it can be. A big corporation is normally heavily dependent upon its brand name for the sale of its products around the world. Where a company miscalculates the strength of public opinion on a given issue, its brand image, and therefore its economic success, can be damaged – as happened, for instance, to Monsanto, a company that sought to promote genetically modified foods into Europe. The reactions of environmental and consumer groups forced the company to abandon its plans and substantially undermined its economic position.

Those in the anti-globalisation movement are surely right to emphasise that the divisions between rich and poor in the world today are unacceptable. The movement has played an important role in forcing this issue on to the agenda of the international community, and making sure that the leaders of the affluent nations listen. But there are two key questions that must be raised. Is it true, as most in the anti-globalisation movement claim, that global economic inequalities are increasing? And if so, is this increase the result of globalisation?

There is intense academic discussion of whether economic inequality is on the increase. The data from many countries are less than wholly reliable, and trends cannot always be inferred with much certainty. Comparisons are often made between countries on a misleading basis. For instance, comparisons are sometimes made between the

GDP of different states without factoring in differences in prices and the cost of living – a more accurate measure.

We cannot really be sure whether world economic inequalities have grown or declined. Some scholars hold that they are on the increase. Many others, including myself, argue the opposite. Economic inequalities between nations and regions, they say, almost certainly increased from about 1860 to 1960, a period during which the Western countries and Japan, under the impact of industrialisation, made a great deal of economic progress, while most other parts of the world did not. But since then, inequality has either stabilised or become reduced.

However, gross generalisations of this sort do not make much sense anyway. There are major differences between different regions of the world when we look at economic trends. Over the past forty years, some less developed countries, especially in Asia, have undergone significant processes of industrialisation. Because they have had much higher growth rates than most Western countries during that period, by definition the overall inequalities between them and the West have declined. Other areas have fared less well. Latin America as a whole, for instance, has made little advance relative to the more industrialised countries. Africa is the continent that has suffered most. In some African countries, living standards have fallen not just in relative terms but in absolute ones too.

When the anti-globalisers blame inequality on globalisation they normally have in mind a much narrower interpretation of globalisation than I argue for in this book – they identify it with the growth of market competition and free trade. Yet even using such a restricted notion, the evidence suggests that these factors favour economic growth and on balance tend to cause inequalities to lessen, not intensify. African countries have experienced problems not because of the effects of globalisation, but on the contrary because they have been left out. The most comprehensive research we have on poor countries shows that, over the past 20 years, those that have opened their economies up to external markets have had average growth rates of 5 per cent. Poor economies that remained closed have had average growth rates of zero per cent.

Inequalities have increased within some of the nations with higher growth rates, but most often because in those countries there was 'equality in poverty' before the occurrence of economic growth. Thus in China inequality has risen. But this increase has happened because initially China was both extremely equal and extremely poor. Over the past three or four decades, hundreds of millions of people in China have escaped from poverty – the most large-scale improvement in living standards ever seen. The numbers of rural poor in China went down from 250 million in 1978 to 34 million in 1999. Not all countries that have achieved significant rises in their level of prosperity have experienced increasing internal inequality. Vietnam, for instance, has had a high rate of economic growth without any deterioration of equality. The level of absolute poverty in Vietnam was reduced by 50 per cent between 1990 and 2000; 98 per cent of the very poorest households became better off in the 1990s.

In making these points I do not want to say that the worries of the anti-globalisers are without foundation. On the contrary, they are real and justified. A retreat from globalisation, however, even if it were possible, would not resolve them. We need to advance globalisation further rather than retard it, but globalisation has to be managed more effectively and equitably than has happened over the past few decades, and the ideological agenda of economic development shifted. As I stress in the text, in most poor countries that have achieved economic success have done much more than just liberalise their trade policy. The idea that economic development can come about purely through the stimulus of market competition is false and even dangerous. A country which opens up its economy to free trade without other social and economic reforms is likely to experience economic deterioration rather than growth. The guiding hand of the state is needed, as are institutional reforms promoting education and the emancipation of women, banking reforms and the fostering of a stable investment climate. These goals are by no means beyond the reach of even very poor countries, as the major advances made in nations such as Botswana and Mozambique show.

Many countries on the margins of the world economy will require help from the rich societies, not only money for investment and technological assistance, but other kinds of knowledge and expertise that can guide institutional reform. The United Nations has declared its aim to halve world poverty by the year 2015. It will take some doing, but given goodwill on the part of the richer societies in the world community, and positive changes in the poorer ones, the ambition can be met.

Anthony Giddens

May 2002

Preface to the first edition

This book started life as the BBC Reith Lectures for the year 1999, broadcast on BBC Radio 4 and the World Service. There is a certain distinction in being the last Reith lecturer of the twentieth century. Given the timing, it seemed to me appropriate to tackle an ambitious set of themes about the state of the world at century's end. I hoped that the lectures would stir up controversy, and such proved to be the case. They were attacked in a gratifying way in newspapers and magazines across the world. Fortunately, they attracted plenty of defenders too.

I called the lectures, and this book, *Runaway World*, because the phrase captures feelings many of us have, living at a time of rapid change. But I am not the first person to have used the term 'runaway world'. I am not even the first Reith lecturer to have employed it. It was the title of the Reith Lectures given by the celebrated anthropologist, Edmund Leach, some quarter of a century ago. However, he put a question mark after his title. I don't think one is needed any more.

Leach recorded his lectures in a studio somewhere in the depths of Broadcasting House, London, as did every contributor until recently. The 1998 lecturer, the historian of war John Keegan, departed from convention by speaking in front of an invited audience. Each lecture was succeeded by a question and answer session. My lectures also followed this format, but they marked a further new departure, because they were the first to be given internationally. The opening lecture and the final one – on globalisation and democracy – were given in London. Those on risk, tradition and the family were recorded in Hong Kong, Delhi and Washington DC respectively. Each lecture provoked a vigorous response from the audiences and I should like to thank all those who took part.

I also want to thank contributors to the Internet debate that was built around the lectures. What we tried to do was to initiate an electronic global conversation about globalisation. Large numbers of people from all corners of the world sent in their comments and criticisms. I hope that they'll forgive me for not being able to respond individually to the points they made and the queries they raised.

Others were involved in a much more continuous way in developing the lectures, and I owe a great debt to them for whatever success the lectures achieved. I should like to mention particularly: James Boyle, Controller of Radio 4; Sir Christopher Bland, Chairman of the BBC; Gwyneth Williams, producer; Charles Sigler, Smita Patel, Gary Wisby, Mark Byford, Mark Smith, Marion Greenwood, Jenny Abramsky, Sue Lynas, Mark Damazer, Sheila Cook and the rest of the BBC production team; the BBC presenters, who did such an able job – Melvyn Bragg, Matt Frei, Mark Tully and Bridget Kendall; Anna Ford, who helped in many ways; from the London School of Economics – Anne de Sayrah, Denise Annett, Miriam Clarke, who did a sterling job typing and retyping the manuscript, Amanda Goodall, Alison Cheevers, Chris Fuller, Fiona Hodgson, Boris Holzer and Reggie Simpson. I am especially grateful to Alena Ledeneva for her advice and support. David Held read several different versions of the manuscript and made many incisive comments.

Anthony Giddens

June 1999

Introduction

'The world is in a rush, and is getting close to its end' – thus spoke one Archbishop Wulfstan, in a sermon given in York, in the year 1014. It is easy to imagine the same sentiments being expressed today. Are the hopes and anxieties of each period merely a carbon copy of previous eras? Is the world in which we live, at the close of the twentieth century, really any different from that of earlier times?

It is. There are good, objective reasons to believe that we are living through a major period of historical transition. Moreover, the changes affecting us aren't confined to any one area of the globe, but stretch almost everywhere.

Our epoch developed under the impact of science, technology and rational thought, having their origins in seventeenth- and eighteenth-century Europe. Western industrial culture was shaped by the Enlightenment – by the writings of thinkers who opposed the influence of religion and dogma, and who wished to replace them with a more reasoned approach to practical life.

The Enlightenment philosophers operated with a simple but apparently very powerful precept. The more we are able rationally to understand the world, and ourselves, they thought, the more we can shape history for our own purposes. We have to free ourselves from the habits and prejudices of the past in order to control the future.

Karl Marx, whose ideas owed a great deal to Enlightenment thought, put the notion very simply. We have to understand history, he argued, in order to make history. Marx and Marxism had a massive influence in the twentieth century under the guidance of this notion.

According to this view, with the further development of science and technology, the world should become more stable and ordered. Even many thinkers who opposed Marx accepted such an idea. The novelist, George Orwell, for example, anticipated a society with too much stability and predictability – in which we would all become tiny cogs in a vast social and economic machine. So did many social thinkers, such as the famous German sociologist, Max Weber.

The world in which we find ourselves today, however, doesn't look or feel much like they predicted it would. Rather than being more and more under our control, it seems out of our control – a runaway world. Moreover, some of the influences that were supposed to make life more certain and predictable for us, including the progress of science and technology, often have quite the opposite effect. Global climate change and its accompanying risks, for example, probably result from our intervention into the environment. They aren't natural phenomena. Science and technology are inevitably involved in our attempts to counter such risks, but they have also contributed to creating them in the first place.

We face risk situations that no one in previous history has had to confront – of which global warming is only one. Many of the new risks and uncertainties affect us no matter where we live, and regardless of how privileged or deprived we are. They are bound up with globalisation, that package of changes which is the subject of this book as a whole. Science and technology have themselves become globalised. It has been calculated that there are more scientists working in the world today than have been involved in the whole history of science previously. But globalisation has a diversity of other dimensions too. It brings into play other forms of risk and uncertainty, especially those involved in the global electronic economy – itself a very recent development. As in the case of science, risk here is double-edged. Risk is closely connected to innovation. It isn't always to be minimised; the active embrace of financial and entrepreneurial risk is the very driving force of the globalising economy.

What globalisation is, and whether it is in any way new, are the focus of intense debate. I discuss this debate in Chapter 1, since much else hangs upon it. Yet the facts of the matter are actually quite clear. Globalisation is restructuring the ways in which we live, and in a very profound manner. It is led from the west, bears the strong imprint of American political and economic power, and is highly uneven in its consequences. But globalisation is not just the dominance of the West over the rest; it affects the United States as it does other countries.

Globalisation also influences everyday life as much as it does events happening on a world scale. That is why this book includes an extended discussion of sexuality, marriage and the family. In most parts of the world, women are staking claim to greater autonomy than in the past and are entering the labour force in large numbers. Such aspects of globalisation are at least as important as those happening in the global market-place. They contribute to the stresses and strains affecting traditional ways of life and cultures in most regions of the world. The traditional family is under threat, is changing, and will change much further. Other traditions, such as those connected with religion, are also experiencing major transformations. Fundamentalism originates from a world of crumbling traditions.

The battleground of the twenty-first century will pit fundamentalism against cosmopolitan tolerance. In a globalising world, where information and images are routinely transmitted across the globe, we are all regularly in contact with others who think differently, and live differently, from ourselves. Cosmopolitans welcome and embrace this cultural complexity. Fundamentalists find it disturbing and dangerous. Whether in the areas of religion, ethnic identity or nationalism, they take refuge in a renewed and purified tradition – and, quite often, violence.

We can legitimately hope that a cosmopolitan outlook will win out. Tolerance of cultural diversity and democracy are closely connected, and democracy is currently spreading world-wide. Globalisation lies behind the expansion of democracy. At the same time, paradoxically, it exposes the limits of the democratic structures which are most familiar, namely the structures of parliamentary democracy. We need to further democratise existing institutions, and to do so in ways that respond to the demands of the global age. We shall never be able to become the masters of our own history, but we can and must find ways of bringing our runaway world to heel.

I

Globalisation

A friend of mine studies village life in central Africa. A few years ago, she paid her first visit to a remote area where she was to carry out her fieldwork. The day she arrived, she was invited to a local home for an evening's entertainment. She expected to find out about the traditional pastimes of this isolated community. Instead, the occasion turned out to be a viewing of *Basic Instinct* on video. The film at that point hadn't even reached the cinemas in London.

Such vignettes reveal something about our world. And what they reveal isn't trivial. It isn't just a matter of people adding modern paraphernalia – videos, television sets, personal computers and so forth – to their existing ways of life. We live in a world of transformations, affecting almost every aspect of what we do. For better or worse, we are being propelled into a global order that no one fully understands, but which is making its effects felt upon all of us.

Globalisation may not be a particularly attractive or elegant word. But absolutely no one who wants to understand our prospects at century's end can ignore it. I travel a lot to speak abroad. I haven't been to a single country recently where globalisation isn't being intensively discussed. In France, the word is *mondialisation*. In Spain and Latin America, it is *globalización*. The Germans say *Globalisierung*.

The global spread of the term is evidence of the very developments to which it refers. Every business guru talks about it. No political speech is complete without reference to it. Yet even in the late 1980s the term was hardly used, either in the academic literature or in everyday language. It has come from nowhere to be almost everywhere.

Given its sudden popularity, we shouldn't be surprised that the meaning of the notion isn't always clear, or that an intellectual reaction has set in against it. Globalisation has something to do with the thesis that we now all live in one world – but in what ways exactly, and is the idea really valid? Different thinkers have taken almost completely opposite views about globalisation in debates that have sprung up over the past few years. Some dispute the whole thing. I'll call them the sceptics.

According to the sceptics, all the talk about

globalisation is only that – just talk. Whatever its benefits, its trials and tribulations, the global economy isn't
especially different from that which existed at previous
periods. The world carries on much the same as it has
done for many years.

Most countries, the sceptics argue, gain only a small
amount of their income from external trade. Moreover,
a good deal of economic exchange is between regions,
rather than being truly world-wide. The countries of the
European Union, for example, mostly trade among
themselves. The same is true of the other main trading
blocs, such as those of Asia–Pacific or North America.

Others take a very different position. I'll label them
the radicals. The radicals argue that not only is globalisation very real, but that its consequences can be felt
everywhere. The global market-place, they say, is much
more developed than even in the 1960s and 1970s and is
indifferent to national borders. Nations have lost most of
the sovereignty they once had, and politicians have lost
most of their capability to influence events. It isn't surprising that no one respects political leaders any more,
or has much interest in what they have to say. The era of
the nation-state is over. Nations, as the Japanese business
writer Kenichi Ohmae puts it, have become mere 'fic-
tions'. Authors such as Ohmae see the economic diffi-
culties of the 1998 Asian crisis as demonstrating the
reality of globalisation, albeit seen from its disruptive side.

The sceptics tend to be on the political left, especially

the old left. For if all of this is essentially a myth, governments can still control economic life and the welfare state remain intact. The notion of globalisation, according to the sceptics, is an ideology put about by free-marketeers who wish to dismantle welfare systems and cut back on state expenditures. What has happened is at most a reversion to how the world was a century ago. In the late nineteenth century there was already an open global economy, with a great deal of trade, including trade in currencies.

Well, who is right in this debate? I think it is the radicals. The level of world trade today is much higher than it ever was before, and involves a much wider range of goods and services. But the biggest difference is in the level of finance and capital flows. Geared as it is to electronic money – money that exists only as digits in computers – the current world economy has no parallels in earlier times.

In the new global electronic economy, fund managers, banks, corporations, as well as millions of individual investors, can transfer vast amounts of capital from one side of the world to another at the click of a mouse. As they do so, they can destabilise what might have seemed rock-solid economies – as happened in the events in Asia.

The volume of world financial transactions is usually measured in US dollars. A million dollars is a lot of money for most people. Measured as a stack of hundred-dollar notes, it would be eight inches high. A billion dollars – in other words, a thousand million – would stand higher than St Paul's Cathedral. A trillion dollars – a million million – would be over 120 miles high, 20 times higher than Mount Everest.

Yet far more than a trillion dollars is now turned over *each day* on global currency markets. This is a massive increase from only the late 1980s, let alone the more distant past. The value of whatever money we may have in our pockets, or our bank accounts, shifts from moment to moment according to fluctuations in such markets.

I would have no hesitation, therefore, in saying that globalisation, as we are experiencing it, is in many respects not only new, but also revolutionary. Yet I don't believe that either the sceptics or the radicals have properly understood either what it is or its implications for us. Both groups see the phenomenon almost solely in economic terms. This is a mistake. Globalisation is political, technological and cultural, as well as economic. It has been influenced above all by developments in systems of communication, dating back only to the late 1960s.

In the mid-nineteenth century, a Massachusetts portrait painter, Samuel Morse, transmitted the first message, 'What hath God wrought?', by electric telegraph. In so doing, he initiated a new phase in world history. Never before could a message be sent without someone going somewhere to carry it. Yet the advent of satellite communications marks every bit as dramatic a break with the past. The first commercial satellite was launched only in 1969. Now there are more than 200 such satellites above the earth, each carrying a vast range of information. For the first time ever, instantaneous communication is possible from one side of the world to the other. Other types of electronic communication, more and more integrated with satellite transmission, have also accelerated over the past few years. No dedicated transatlantic or transpacific cables existed at all until the late 1950s. The first held fewer than 100 voice paths. Those of today carry more than a million.

On 1 February 1999, about 150 years after Morse invented his system of dots and dashes, Morse Code finally disappeared from the world stage. It was discontinued as a means of communication for the sea. In its place has come a system using satellite technology, whereby any ship in distress can be pinpointed immediately. Most countries prepared for the transition some while before. The French, for example, stopped using Morse Code in their local waters in 1997, signing off with a Gallic flourish: 'Calling all. This is our last cry before our eternal silence'.

Instantaneous electronic communication isn't just a way in which news or information is conveyed more quickly. Its existence alters the very texture of our lives, rich and poor alike. When the image of Nelson Mandela may be more familiar to us than the face of our next-

11

door neighbour, something has changed in the nature of our everyday experience.

Nelson Mandela is a global celebrity, and celebrity itself is largely a product of new communications technology. The reach of media technologies is growing with each wave of innovation. It took 40 years for radio in the United States to gain an audience of 50 million. The same number was using personal computers only 15 years after the personal computer was introduced. It needed a mere 4 years, after it was made available, for 50 million Americans to be regularly using the Internet.

It is wrong to think of globalisation as just concerning the big systems, like the world financial order. Globalisation isn't only about what is 'out there', remote and far away from the individual. It is an 'in here' phenomenon too, influencing intimate and personal aspects of our lives. The debate about family values, for example, that is going on in many countries might seem far removed from globalising influences. It isn't. Traditional family systems are becoming transformed, or are under strain, in many parts of the world, particularly as women stake claim to greater equality. There has never before been a society, so far as we know from the historical record, in which women have been even approximately equal to men. This is a truly global revolution in everyday life, whose consequences are being felt around the world in spheres from work to politics.

Globalisation thus is a complex set of processes, not a

single one. And these operate in a contradictory or oppositional fashion. Most people think of globalisation as simply 'pulling away' power or influence from local communities and nations into the global arena. And indeed this is one of its consequences. Nations do lose some of the economic power they once had. Yet it also has an opposite effect. Globalisation not only pulls upwards, but also pushes downwards, creating new pressures for local autonomy. The American sociologist Daniel Bell describes this very well when he says that the nation becomes not only too small to solve the big problems, but also too large to solve the small ones.

Globalisation is the reason for the revival of local cultural identities in different parts of the world. If one asks, for example, why the Scots want more independence in the UK, or why there is a strong separatist movement in Quebec, the answer is not to be found only in their cultural history. Local nationalisms spring up as a response to globalising tendencies, as the hold of older nation-states weakens.

Globalisation also squeezes sideways. It creates new economic and cultural zones within and across nations. Examples are the Hong Kong region, northern Italy, and Silicon Valley in California. Or consider the Barcelona region. The area around Barcelona in northern Spain extends into France. Catalonia, where Barcelona is located, is closely integrated into the European Union. It is part of Spain, yet also looks outwards.

These changes are being propelled by a range of factors, some structural, others more specific and historical. Economic influences are certainly among the driving forces – especially the global financial system. Yet they aren't like forces of nature. They have been shaped by technology, and cultural diffusion, as well as by the decisions of governments to liberalise and deregulate their national economies.

The collapse of Soviet communism has added further weight to such developments, since no significant group of countries any longer stands outside. That collapse wasn't just something that just happened to occur. Globalisation explains both why and how Soviet communism met its end. The former Soviet Union and the East European countries were comparable to the West in terms of growth rates until somewhere around the early 1970s. After that point, they fell rapidly behind. Soviet communism, with its emphasis upon state-run enterprise and heavy industry, could not compete in the global electronic economy. The ideological and cultural control upon which communist political authority was based similarly could not survive in an era of global media.

The Soviet and the East European regimes were unable to prevent the reception of Western radio and television broadcasts. Television played a direct role in the 1989 revolutions, which have rightly been called the first 'television revolutions'. Street protests taking place in one country were watched by television audiences in others, large numbers of whom then took to the streets themselves.

Globalisation, of course, isn't developing in an even-handed way, and is by no means wholly benign in its consequences. To many living outside Europe and North America, it looks uncomfortably like Westernisation – or, perhaps, Americanisation, since the US is now the sole superpower, with a dominant economic, cultural and military position in the global order. Many of the most visible cultural expressions of globalisation are American – Coca-Cola, McDonald's, CNN.

Most of the giant multinational companies are based in the US too. Those that aren't all come from the rich countries, not the poorer areas of the world. A pessimistic view of globalisation would consider it largely an affair of the industrial North, in which the developing societies of the South play little or no active part. It would see it as destroying local cultures, widening world inequalities and worsening the lot of the impoverished. Globalisation, some argue, creates a world of winners and losers, a few on the fast track to prosperity, the majority condemned to a life of misery and despair.

Indeed, the statistics are daunting. The share of the poorest fifth of the world's population in global income has dropped, from 2.3 per cent to 1.4 per cent between 1989 and 1998. The proportion taken by the richest fifth, on the other hand, has risen. In sub-Saharan Africa, 20 countries have lower incomes per head in real terms than they had in the late 1970s. In many less developed countries, safety and environmental regulations are low or virtually non-existent. Some transnational companies sell goods there that are controlled or banned in the industrial countries – poor-quality medical drugs, destructive pesticides or high tar and nicotine content cigarettes. Rather than a global village, one might say, this is more like global pillage.

Along with ecological risk, to which it is related, expanding inequality is the most serious problem facing world society. It will not do, however, merely to blame it on the wealthy. It is fundamental to my argument that globalisation today is only partly Westernisation. Of course the Western nations, and more generally the industrial countries, still have far more influence over world affairs than do the poorer states. But globalisation is becoming increasingly decentred – not under the control of any group of nations, and still less of the large corporations. Its effects are felt as much in Western countries as elsewhere.

This is true of the global financial system, and of changes affecting the nature of government itself. What one could call 'reverse colonisation' is becoming more and more common. Reverse colonisation means that non-Western countries influence developments in the West. Examples abound – such as the latinising of Los Angeles, the emergence of a globally oriented high-tech

16

sector in India, or the selling of Brazilian television programmes to Portugal.

Is globalisation a force promoting the general good? The question can't be answered in a simple way, given the complexity of the phenomenon. People who ask it, and who blame globalisation for deepening world inequalities, usually have in mind economic globalisation and, within that, free trade. Now, it is surely obvious that free trade is not an unalloyed benefit. This is especially so as concerns the less developed countries. Opening up a country, or regions within it, to free trade can undermine a local subsistence economy. An area that becomes dependent upon a few products sold on world markets is very vulnerable to shifts in prices as well as to technological change.

Trade always needs a framework of institutions, as do other forms of economic development. Markets cannot be created by purely economic means, and how far a given economy should be exposed to the world marketplace must depend upon a range of criteria. Yet to oppose economic globalisation, and to opt for economic protectionism, would be a misplaced tactic for rich and poor nations alike. Protectionism may be a necessary strategy at some times and in some countries. In my view, for example, Malaysia was correct to introduce controls in 1998, to stem the flood of capital from the country. But more permanent forms of protectionism will not help the development of the poor countries,

and among the rich would lead to warring trade blocs.
The debates about globalisation I mentioned at the
beginning have concentrated mainly upon its implications for the nation-state. Are nation-states, and hence
national political leaders, still powerful, or are they
becoming largely irrelevant to the forces shaping the
world? Nation-states are indeed still powerful and political leaders have a large role to play in the world. Yet at
the same time the nation-state is being reshaped before
our eyes. National economic policy can't be as effective
as it once was. More importantly, nations have to rethink
their identities now the older forms of geopolitics are
becoming obsolete. Although this is a contentious point,
I would say that, following the dissolving of the Cold
War, most nations no longer have enemies. Who are the
enemies of Britain, or France, or Brazil? The war in
Kosovo didn't pit nation against nation. It was a conflict
between old-style territorial nationalism and a new, eth-
ically driven interventionalism.

Nations today face risks and dangers rather than enemies, a massive shift in their very nature. It isn't only of
the nation that such comments could be made. Everywhere we look, we see institutions that appear the same
as they used to be from the outside, and carry the same
names, but inside have become quite different. We continue to talk of the nation, the family, work, tradition,
nature, as if they were all the same as in the past. They are
not. The outer shell remains, but inside they have

18

changed – and this is happening not only in the US, Britain, or France, but almost everywhere. They are what I call 'shell institutions'. They are institutions that have become inadequate to the tasks they are called upon to perform.

As the changes I have described in this chapter gather weight, they are creating something that has never existed before, a global cosmopolitan society. We are the first generation to live in this society, whose contours we can as yet only dimly see. It is shaking up our existing ways of life, no matter where we happen to be. This is not – at least at the moment – a global order driven by collective human will. Instead, it is emerging in an anarchic, haphazard, fashion, carried along by a mixture of influences.

It is not settled or secure, but fraught with anxieties, as well as scarred by deep divisions. Many of us feel in the grip of forces over which we have no power. Can we reimpose our will upon them? I believe we can. The powerlessness we experience is not a sign of personal failings, but reflects the incapacities of our institutions. We need to reconstruct those we have, or create new ones. For globalisation is not incidental to our lives today. It is a shift in our very life circumstances. It is the way we now live.

2

Risk

July 1998 was possibly the hottest month in world history and 1998 as a whole may have been the hottest year. Heat waves caused havoc in many areas of the northern hemisphere. In Eilat, in Israel, for example, temperatures rose to almost 46 degrees centigrade, while water consumption in the country went up by 40 per cent. Texas, in the United States, experienced temperatures not far short of this. For the first eight months of the year, each month topped the record for that month. A short while later, however, in some of the areas affected by the heat waves, snow fell in places that had never seen it before.

Are temperature shifts like this the result of human interference with the world's climate? We can't be sure, but we have to admit the possibility that they might be, together with the increased numbers of hurricanes, typhoons and storms that have been noted in recent years. As a consequence of global industrial development, we may have altered the world's climate, and damaged a great deal more of our earthly habitat besides. We don't know what further changes will result, or the dangers they will bring in their train.

We can make sense of these issues by saying that they are all bound up with *risk*. I hope to persuade you that this apparently simple notion unlocks some of the most basic characteristics of the world in which we now live.

At first sight, the concept of risk might seem to have no specific relevance to our times, as compared to previous ages. After all, haven't people always had to face their fair share of risks? Life for the majority in the European Middle Ages was nasty, brutish and short – as it is for many in poorer areas of the world now.

But here we come across something really interesting. Apart from some marginal contexts, in the Middle Ages there was no concept of risk. Nor, so far as I have been able to find out, was there in most other traditional cultures. The idea of risk appears to have taken hold in the sixteenth and seventeenth centuries, and was first coined by Western explorers as they set off on their voyages across the world. The word 'risk' seems to have come into English through Spanish or Portuguese, where it was used to refer to sailing into uncharted waters. Originally, in other words, it had an orientation to space. Later, it became transferred to time, as used in banking and investment, to mean calculation of the probable consequences of investment decisions for borrowers and lenders. It subsequently came to refer to a wide range of other situations of uncertainty.

The notion of risk, I should point out, is inseparable from the ideas of probability and uncertainty. A person can't be said to be running a risk where an outcome is 100 per cent certain.

There is an old joke that makes this point rather neatly. A man jumps from the top of a hundred-storey skyscraper. As he passes each floor, on his way down, the people inside hear him saying: 'so far so good', 'so far so good', 'so far so good' ... He acts as though he is making a risk calculation, but the outcome is in fact determined.

Traditional cultures didn't have a concept of risk because they didn't need one. Risk isn't the same as hazard or danger. Risk refers to hazards that are actively assessed in relation to future possibilities. It comes into wide usage only in a society that is future oriented – which sees the future precisely as a territory to be conquered or colonised. Risk presumes a society that actively tries to break away from its past – the prime characteristic, indeed, of modern industrial civilisation.

All previous cultures, including the great early civilisations of the world, such as Rome, or traditional China, have lived primarily in the past. They have used the ideas of fate, luck or the will of the gods where we now tend to substitute risk. In traditional cultures, if someone meets with an accident or, conversely, prospers – well, it is just one of those things, or it is what the gods and spirits intended. Some cultures have denied the idea of chance happenings altogether. The Azande, an African tribe, believe that when a misfortune befalls someone it is the result of sorcery. If an individual falls ill, for example, it is because an enemy has been practising black magic.

Such views, of course, don't disappear completely with modernisation. Magical notions, concepts of fate and cosmology still have a hold. But often they continue on as superstitions, in which people only half believe, and follow in a somewhat embarrassed way. They use them to back up decisions of a more calculative nature. Gamblers, and this includes gamblers on the stock exchange, mostly have rituals that psychologically reduce the uncertainties they must confront. The same applies to many risks that we can't help running, since being alive at all is by definition a risky business. It isn't in any way surprising that people still consult astrologers, especially at vital points of their lives.

Yet acceptance of risk is also the condition of excitement and adventure – think of the pleasures some people get from the risks of gambling, driving fast, sexual adventurism, or the plunge of a fairground roller-coaster. Moreover, a positive embrace of risk is the very source of that energy which creates wealth in a modern economy.

The two aspects of risk – its negative and positive sides – appear from the early days of modern industrial society. Risk is the mobilising dynamic of a society bent on change, that wants to determine its own future rather than leaving it to religion, tradition, or the vagaries of nature. Modern capitalism differs from all previous forms of economic system in terms of its attitudes towards the future. Previous types of market enterprise were irregular or partial. The activities of merchants and traders, for example, never made much dent in the basic structure of traditional civilisations, which all remained heavily agricultural and rural.

Modern capitalism embeds itself into the future by calculating future profit and loss, and therefore risk, as a continuous process. This couldn't be done until the invention of double entry bookkeeping in the fifteenth century in Europe, which made it possible to track in a precise way how money can be invested to make more money. Many risks, of course, such as those affecting health, we do wish to reduce as far as we can. This is why, from its origins, the notion of risk is accompanied by the rise of insurance. We shouldn't think only of private or commercial insurance here. The welfare state, whose development can be traced back to the Elizabethan poor laws in England, is essentially a risk management system. It is designed to protect against hazards that were once treated as at the disposition of the gods – sickness, disablement, job loss and old age.

Insurance is the baseline against which people are prepared to take risks. It is the basis of security where fate has been ousted by an active engagement with the future. Like the idea of risk, modern forms of insurance began with seafaring. The earliest marine insurances were written in the sixteenth century. A London company first underwrote an overseas risk in 1782. Lloyds of London soon after took a leading position in the emerging insurance industry, a position that it has sustained for two centuries.

Insurance is conceivable only where we believe in a humanly engineered future. It is one of the means of doing that engineering. Insurance is about providing security, but it is actually parasitic upon risk and people's attitudes towards it. Those who provide insurance, whether in the shape of private insurance or state welfare systems, are essentially simply redistributing risk. If someone takes out fire insurance against his or her house burning down, the risk doesn't go away. The householder trades off the risk to the insurer in exchange for payment. The trading and off-loading of risk isn't just a casual feature of a capitalist economy. Capitalism is actually unthinkable and unworkable without it.

For these reasons, the idea of risk has always been involved in modernity, but I want to argue that in the current period risk assumes a new and peculiar importance. Risk was supposed to be a way of regulating the future, of normalising it and bringing it under our dominion. Things haven't turned out that way. Our very attempts to control the future tend to rebound upon us, forcing us to look for different ways of relating to uncertainty.

The best way to explain what is going on is to make a distinction between two types of risk. One I shall call external risk. External risk is risk experienced as coming from the outside, from the fixities of tradition or nature. I want to distinguish this from manufactured risk, by which I mean risk created by the very impact of our developing knowledge upon the world. Manufactured risk refers to risk situations which we have very little historical experience of confronting. Most environmental risks, such as those connected with global warming, fall into this category. They are directly influenced by the intensifying globalisation I discussed in Chapter 1.

The best way I can clarify the distinction between the two kinds of risk is as follows. In all traditional cultures, one could say, and in industrial society right up to the threshold of the present day, human beings worried about the risks coming from external nature – from bad harvests, floods, plagues or famines. At a certain point, however – very recently in historical terms – we started worrying less about what nature can do to us, and more about what we have done to nature. This marks the transition from the predominance of external risk to that of manufactured risk.

Who are the 'we' here, doing the worrying? Well, I think now it is all of us, regardless of whether we are in the richer or poorer areas of the world. At the same time, it is obvious that there is a division that by and large separates the affluent regions from the rest. Many more 'traditional' risks, of the sort just mentioned – such as the risk of famine when the harvest is bad – still exist in poorer countries, overlapping with the new risks.

Our society lives after the end of nature. The end of nature doesn't mean, obviously, that the physical world or physical processes cease to exist. It refers to the fact that there are few aspects of our surrounding material environment that haven't been in some way affected by human intervention. Much of what used to be natural isn't completely natural any more, although we can't always be sure where the one stops and the other begins. In 1998 there were big floods in China, in which many people lost their lives. The flooding of the major rivers has been a recurrent part of Chinese history. Were these particular floods more of the same, or were they influenced by global climate change? No one knows, but there are some unusual features of the floods that suggest their causes were not wholly natural.

Manufactured risk doesn't only concern nature – or what used to be nature. It penetrates into other areas of life too. Take, for example, marriage and the family, now undergoing profound changes in the industrial countries and to some extent world-wide. Two or three generations ago, when people got married, they knew what it was they were doing. Marriage, largely fixed by tradition and custom, was akin to a state of nature – as of course remains true in many countries. Where traditional ways of doing things are dissolving, however, when people marry or form relationships, there is an important sense in which they don't know what they are doing, because the institutions of marriage and the family have changed so much. Here individuals are striking out afresh, like pioneers. It is inevitable in such situations, whether they know it or not, that they start thinking more and more in terms of risk. They have to confront personal futures that are much more open than in the past, with all the opportunities and hazards this brings.

As manufactured risk expands, there is a new riskiness to risk. The rise of the idea of risk, as I pointed out earlier, was closely tied to the possibility of calculation. Most forms of insurance are based directly upon this connection. Every time someone steps into a car, for instance, one can calculate that person's chances of being involved in an accident. This is actuarial prediction – there is a long time-series to go on. Situations of manufactured risk aren't like this. We simply don't know what the level of risk is, and in many cases we won't know for sure until it is too late.

Not long ago (1996) was the tenth anniversary of the accident at the Chernobyl nuclear station in the

Ukraine. No one knows what its long-term consequences will be. There might or might not be a stored-up disaster to health due to happen some while from now. Exactly the same is true of the BSE episode in the UK – the outbreak of so-called mad cow disease – in terms of its implications for humans. At the moment, we can't be sure whether at some point many more people than at present will fall ill.

Or consider where we stand with world climate change. Most scientists well versed in the field believe that global warming is occurring and that measures should be taken against it. Yet only in the mid-1970s, orthodox scientific opinion was that the world was in a phase of global cooling. Much the same evidence that was deployed to support the hypothesis of global cooling is now brought into play to bolster that of global warming – heat waves, cold spells, unusual types of weather. Is global warming occurring, and does it have human origins? Probably – but we won't, and can't, be completely sure until it is too late.

In these circumstances, there is a new moral climate of politics, marked by a push and pull between accusations of scaremongering on the one hand, and of cover-ups on the other. If anyone – government official, scientific expert or researcher – takes a given risk seriously, he or she must proclaim it. It must be widely publicised because people must be persuaded that the risk is real – a fuss must be made about it. Yet if a fuss is indeed created and the risk turns out to be minimal, those involved will be accused of scaremongering.

Suppose, however, that the authorities initially decide that the risk is not very great, as the British government did in the case of contaminated beef. In this instance, the government first of all said: we've got the backing of scientists here; there isn't a significant risk, and anyone who wants to can continue eating beef without any worries. In such situations, if events turn out otherwise – as in fact they did – the authorities will be accused of a cover-up – as indeed they were.

Things are even more complex than these examples suggest. Paradoxically, scaremongering may be necessary to reduce risks we face – yet if it is successful, it appears as just that, scaremongering. The case of AIDS is an example. Governments and experts made great public play with the risks associated with unsafe sex, to get people to change their sexual behaviour. Partly as a consequence, in the developed countries, AIDS did not spread as much as was originally predicted. Then the response was: why were you scaring everyone like that? Yet as we know from its continuing global spread, they were – and are – entirely right to do so.

This sort of paradox becomes routine in contemporary society, but there is no easily available way of dealing with it. For as I mentioned earlier, in most situations of manufactured risk, even whether there are risks at all is likely to be disputed. We cannot know beforehand when we are actually scaremongering and when we are not.

Our relationship to science and technology today is different from that characteristic of earlier times. In Western society, for some two centuries, science functioned as a sort of tradition. Scientific knowledge was supposed to overcome tradition, but actually in a way became one in its own right. It was something that most people respected, but was external to their activities. Lay people 'took' opinions from the experts.

The more science and technology intrude into our lives, and do so on a global level, the less this perspective holds. Most of us – including government authorities and politicians – have, and have to have, a much more active or engaged relationship with science and technology than used to be the case.

We cannot simply 'accept' the findings which scientists produce, if only because scientists so frequently disagree with one another, particularly in situations of manufactured risk. And everyone now recognises the essentially mobile character of science. Whenever someone decides what to eat, what to have for breakfast, whether to drink decaffeinated or ordinary coffee, that person takes a decision in the context of conflicting and changeable scientific and technological information.

Consider red wine. As with other alcoholic drinks, red wine was once thought harmful to health. Research then indicated that drinking red wine in reasonable quantities protects against heart disease. Subsequently it was found that any form of alcohol will do, but it is protective only for people above age 40. Who knows what the next set of findings will show?

Some say that the most effective way to cope with the rise of manufactured risk is to limit responsibility by adopting the so-called 'precautionary principle'. The notion of the precautionary principle first emerged in Germany in the early 1980s, in the context of the ecological debates that were carried on there. At its simplest, it proposes that action on environmental issues (and, by inference, other forms of risk) should be taken even though there is insecure scientific evidence about them. Thus in the 1980s, in several European countries, programmes were initiated to counter acid rain, whereas in Britain lack of conclusive evidence was used to justify inactivity about this and other pollution problems too.

Yet the precautionary principle isn't always helpful or even applicable as a means of coping with problems of risk and responsibility. The precept of 'staying close to nature', or of limiting innovation rather than embracing it, can't always apply. The reason is that the balance of benefits and dangers from scientific and technological advance, and other forms of social change too, is imponderable. Take as an example the controversy over genetically modified foods. Genetically modified crops are already growing on 35 million hectares of land across the world – an area 1.5 times the size of Britain. Most are being grown in North America and China. Crops include soya, maize, cotton and potatoes.

No more obvious situation could be found where nature is no longer nature. The risks involve a number of unknowns – or, if I can put it this way, known unknowns, because the world has a pronounced tendency to surprise us. There may be other consequences that no one has yet anticipated. One type of risk is that the crops may carry medium- or long-term health hazards. After all, a good deal of gene technology is essentially new, different from older methods of cross-breeding.

Another possibility is that genes incorporated into crops to increase resistance to pests might spread to other plants – creating 'super weeds'. This in turn could pose a threat to biodiversity in the environment.

Since pressure to grow, and consume, genetically modified crops is partly driven by sheer commercial interests, wouldn't it be sensible to impose a global ban on them? Even supposing such a ban were feasible, things – as ever – are not so simple. The intensive agriculture widely practised today is not indefinitely sustainable. It uses large amounts of chemical fertilisers and insecticides, destructive of the environment. We can't go back to more traditional modes of farming and still hope to feed the world's population. Bioengineered crops could reduce the use of chemical pollutants, and hence help resolve these problems.

Whichever way you look at it, we are caught up in risk management. With the spread of manufactured risk, governments can't pretend such management isn't their business. And they need to collaborate, since very few new-style risks have anything to do with the borders of nations.

But neither, as ordinary individuals, can we ignore these new risks – or wait for definitive scientific evidence to arrive. As consumers, each of us has to decide whether to try to avoid genetically modified products or not. These risks, and the dilemmas surrounding them, have entered deeply into our everyday lives.

Let me move towards some conclusions and at the same time try to make sure my arguments are clear. Our age is not more dangerous – not more risky – than those of earlier generations, but the balance of risks and dangers has shifted. We live in a world where hazards created by ourselves are as, or more, threatening than those that come from the outside. Some of these are genuinely catastrophic, such as global ecological risk, nuclear proliferation or the meltdown of the world economy. Others affect us as individuals much more directly, for instance those involved in diet, medicine or even marriage.

An era such as ours will inevitably breed religious revivalism and diverse New Age philosophies, which turn against a scientific outlook. Some ecological thinkers have become hostile to science, and even to rational thought more generally, because of ecological risks. This isn't an attitude that makes much sense. We wouldn't even know about these risks without scientific analysis. However, our relationship to science, for reasons already given, won't and can't be the same as in previous times.

We do not currently possess institutions which allow us to monitor technological change, nationally or globally. The BSE debacle in Britain and elsewhere might have been avoided if a public dialogue had been established about technological change and its problematic consequences. More public means of engaging with science and technology wouldn't do away with the quandary of scaremongering versus cover-ups, but might allow us to reduce some of its more damaging consequences.

Finally, there can be no question of merely taking a negative attitude towards risk. Risk always needs to be disciplined, but active risk-taking is a core element of a dynamic economy and an innovative society. Living in a global age means coping with a diversity of new situations of risk. We may need quite often to be bold rather than cautious in supporting scientific innovation or other forms of change. After all, one root of the term 'risk' in the original Portuguese means 'to dare'.

3

Tradition

When Scots get together to celebrate their national identity, they do so in ways steeped in tradition. Men wear the kilt, with each clan having its own tartan, and their ceremonials are accompanied by the wail of the bagpipes. By means of these symbols, they show their loyalty to ancient rituals – rituals whose origins go far back into antiquity.

Except for the fact that they don't. Along with most other symbols of Scottishness, all these are quite recent creations. The short kilt seems to have been invented by an English industrialist from Lancashire, Thomas Rawlinson, in the early eighteenth century. He set out to alter the existing dress of Highlanders to make it convenient for workmen.

Kilts were a product of the industrial revolution. The

aim was not to preserve time-honoured customs, but the opposite − to bring the Highlanders out of the heather and into the factory. The kilt didn't start life as the national dress of Scotland. The Lowlanders, who made up the large majority of Scots, saw Highland dress as a barbaric form of clothing, which most looked on with some contempt. Similarly, many of the clan tartans worn now were devised during the Victorian period, by enterprising tailors who correctly saw a market in them. Much of what we think of as traditional, and steeped in the mists of time, is actually a product at most of the last couple of centuries, and is often much more recent than that. The case of the Scottish kilt comes from a celebrated volume by the historians Eric Hobsbawm and Terence Ranger, called *The Invention of Tradition.* They give examples of invented traditions from a variety of different countries, including colonial India.

The British set up an archaeological survey in the 1860s to identify the great monuments of India and to preserve Indian 'heritage'. Believing local arts and crafts to be in decline, they collected together artefacts to put in museums. Before 1860, for example, Indian soldiers and the British both wore Western-style uniforms. But in the eyes of the British, Indians had to look like Indians. The dress uniforms were modified to include turbans, sashes and tunics regarded as 'authentic'. Some of the traditions they invented, or half invented, continue on in the country today, although of course others were later rejected.

Tradition and custom – these have been the stuff of most people's lives for most of human history. Yet it is remarkable how little interest scholars and thinkers tend to show in them. There are endless discussions of modernisation and what it means to be modern, but few indeed about tradition. When I was researching for this chapter, I came across dozens of academic books in English with 'modernity' in the title. Indeed, I have written a few myself – but I could discover only a couple of books specifically about tradition.

It was the eighteenth-century Enlightenment in Europe that gave tradition a bad name. One of its major figures, the Baron d'Holbach, put things this way:

> Instructors have long enough fixed men's eyes upon heaven, let them now turn them upon earth. Fatigued with an inconceivable theology, ridiculous fables, impenetrable mysteries, puerile ceremonies, let the human mind apply itself to the study of nature, to intelligible objects, sensible truths, and useful knowledge. Let the vain chimeras of men be removed, and reasonable opinions will soon come of themselves, into those heads which were thought to be forever destined to error.

It is clear that d'Holbach never intended a serious engagement with tradition and its role in society. Tradition here is merely the shadow side of modernity, an implausible construct that can be easily brushed aside. If we are really to get to grips with tradition, we can't treat it merely as folly. The linguistic roots of the word 'tradition' are old. The English word has its origins in the Latin term *tradere*, which meant to transmit, or give something to another for safekeeping. *Tradere* was originally used in the context of Roman law, where it referred to the laws of inheritance. Property that passed from one generation to another was supposed to be given in trust – the inheritor had obligations to protect and nurture it.

It might seem that the notion of tradition, unlike kilts and bagpipes, has been around for many centuries. Once more, appearances are deceptive. The term 'tradition' as it is used today is actually a product of the past two hundred years in Europe. Just like the concept of risk, which I talked about in the previous chapter, in medieval times there was no generic notion of tradition. There was no call for such a word, precisely because tradition and custom were everywhere.

The idea of tradition, then, is itself a creation of modernity. That doesn't mean that one shouldn't use it in relation to premodern or non-Western societies, but it does imply that we should approach the discussion of tradition with some care. By identifying tradition with dogma and ignorance, the Enlightenment thinkers sought to justify their absorption with the new.

Disentangling ourselves from the prejudices of the

Enlightenment, how should we understand 'tradition'? We can make a good start by going back to invented traditions. Invented traditions and customs, Hobsbawm and Ranger suggest, aren't genuine ones. They are contrived, rather than growing up spontaneously; they are used as a means of power; and they haven't existed since time immemorial. Whatever continuity they imply with the long-term past is largely false.

I would turn their argument on its head. All traditions, I would say, are invented traditions. No traditional societies were wholly traditional, and traditions and customs have been invented for a diversity of reasons. We shouldn't suppose that the conscious construction of tradition is found only in the modern period. Moreover, traditions always incorporate power, whether they are constructed in a deliberate way or not. Kings, emperors, priests and others have long invented traditions to suit themselves and to legitimise their rule.

It is a myth to think of traditions as impervious to change. Traditions evolve over time, but also can be quite suddenly altered or transformed. If I can put it this way, they are invented and reinvented.

Some traditions, of course, such as those associated with the great religions, have lasted for hundreds of years. There are core prescriptions of Islam, for instance, that nearly all Muslim believers would hold to, and which have remained recognisably the same over a very long period. Yet whatever continuity there is in such doctrines goes along with many changes, even revolutionary changes, in how they are interpreted and acted upon. There is no such thing as a completely pure tradition. Like all the other world religions, Islam drew upon a dazzling variety of cultural resources – that is, other traditions. The same was true of the Ottoman empire more generally, which across the years incorporated Arab, Persian, Greek, Roman, Berber, Turkish and Indian influences, among others.

But it is simply wrong to suppose that for a given set of symbols or practices to be traditional, they must have existed for centuries. The Christmas address by the monarch, which is broadcast every year in Britain, has become a tradition. Yet it started only in 1932. Endurance over time is not the key defining feature of tradition, or of its more diffuse cousin, custom. The distinguishing characteristics of tradition are ritual and repetition. Traditions are always properties of groups, communities or collectivities. Individuals may follow traditions and customs, but traditions are not a quality of individual behaviour in the way habits are.

What is distinctive about tradition is that it defines a kind of truth. For someone following a traditional practice, questions don't have to be asked about alternatives. However much it may change, tradition provides a framework for action that can go largely unquestioned. Traditions usually have guardians – wise men, priests, sages. Guardians are not the same as experts. They get their position and power from the fact that only they are capable of interpreting tradition's ritual truth. Only they can decipher the real meanings of the sacred texts or the other symbols involved in the communal rituals.

The Enlightenment set out to destroy the authority of tradition. It only partially succeeded. Traditions remained strong for a long while in most of modern Europe and even more firmly entrenched across most of the rest of the world. Many traditions were reinvented and others were newly instituted. There was a concerted attempt from some sectors of society to protect or adapt the old traditions. After all, this is basically what conservative philosophies have been, and are, all about. Tradition is perhaps the most basic concept of conservatism, since conservatives believe that it contains stored-up wisdom.

A further reason for the persistence of tradition in the industrial countries was that the institutional changes signalled by modernity were largely confined to public institutions – especially government and the economy. Traditional ways of doing things tended to persist, or be re-established, in many other areas of life, including everyday life. One could even say there was a sort of symbiosis between modernity and tradition. In most countries, for example, the family, sexuality and the divisions between the sexes remained heavily saturated with tradition and custom.

Two basic changes are happening today under the

impact of globalisation. In western countries, not only public institutions but also everyday life are becoming opened up from the hold of tradition. And other societies across the world that remained more traditional are becoming detraditionalised. I take it that this is at the core of the emerging global cosmopolitan society I have spoken of previously.

This is a society living after the end of nature. Few aspects of the physical world, in other words, are any longer just natural – unaffected by human intervention. It is also a society living after the end of tradition. The end of tradition doesn't mean that tradition disappears, as the Enlightenment thinkers wanted. On the contrary, in different versions it continues to flourish everywhere. But less and less – if I can put it in this fashion – is it tradition lived in the traditional way. The traditional way means defending traditional activities through their own ritual and symbolism – defending tradition through its internal claims to truth.

A world where modernisation is not confined to one geographical area, but makes itself felt globally, has a number of consequences for tradition. Tradition and science sometimes mingle in odd and interesting ways. Consider, for instance, the much discussed episode that happened in India in 1995, when the deities in some Hindu shrines appeared to drink milk. On the same day, several million people, not only in India but throughout the world, tried to offer milk to a divine image. Denis

Vidal, an anthropologist who has written about this phenomenon, remarks:

> by manifesting themselves simultaneously in every country of the world inhabited by Indians, the Hindu deities may have succeeded in performing the first ever miracle in tune with an era haunted by the slogan of globalisation.

Just as interestingly, it was widely felt – by believers as well as non-believers – that scientific experiments were needed to authenticate the miracle. Science was enlisted in the service of faith.

Tradition in such an example isn't only still alive, it is resurgent. Yet traditions also often succumb to modernity, and are doing so in some situations all over the world. Tradition that is drained of its content, and commercialised, becomes either heritage or kitsch – the trinkets bought in the airport store. As developed by the heritage industry, heritage is tradition repackaged as spectacle. The refurbished buildings at tourist sites may look splendid, and the refurbishment may even be authentic down to the last detail. But the heritage that is thereby protected is severed from the lifeblood of tradition, which is its connection with the experience of everyday life.

In my view, it is entirely rational to recognise that traditions are needed in society. We shouldn't accept the Enlightenment idea that the world should rid itself of tradition altogether. Traditions are needed, and will always persist, because they give continuity and form to life. Take academic life, as an example. Everyone in the academic world works within traditions. Even academic disciplines as a whole, like economics, sociology or philosophy, have traditions. The reason is that no one could work in a wholly eclectic fashion. Without intellectual traditions, ideas would have no focus or direction.

However, it is part of academic life continually to explore the limits of such traditions, and foster active interchange between them. Tradition can perfectly well be defended in a non-traditional way – and that should be its future. Ritual, ceremonial and repetition have an important social role, something understood and acted upon by most organisations, including governments. Traditions will continue to be sustained in so far as they can effectively be justified – not in terms of their own internal rituals, but as compared to other traditions or ways of doing things.

This is true even of religious traditions. Religion is normally associated with the idea of faith, a sort of emotional leap into belief. Yet in a cosmopolitan world, more people than ever before are regularly in contact with others who think differently from them. They are required to justify their beliefs, in an implicit way at least, both to themselves and others. There cannot but be a large dollop of rationality in the persistence of religious rituals and observances in a detraditionalising society. And this is exactly as it should be.

As tradition changes its role, however, new dynamics are introduced into our lives. These can be summarised as a push and pull between autonomy of action and compulsiveness on the one hand, and between cosmopolitanism and fundamentalism on the other. Where tradition has retreated, we are forced to live in a more open and reflective way. Autonomy and freedom can replace the hidden power of tradition with more open discussion and dialogue. But these freedoms bring other problems in their wake. A society living on the other side of nature and tradition – as nearly all Western countries now do – is one that calls for decision making, in everyday life as elsewhere. The dark side of decision making is the rise of addictions and compulsions. Something really intriguing, but also disturbing, is going on here. It is mostly confined to the developed countries, but is becoming seen among more affluent groups elsewhere too. What I am speaking about is the spread of the idea and the reality of addiction. The notion of addiction was originally applied exclusively to alcoholism and drug-taking. But now any area of activity can become invaded by it. One can be addicted to work, exercise, food, sex – or even love. The reason is that these activities, and other parts of life too, are much less structured by tradition and custom than once they were.

Like tradition, addiction is about the influence of the past upon the present; and as in the case of tradition, repetition has a key role. The past in question is individual rather than collective, and the repetition is driven by anxiety. I would see addiction as frozen autonomy. Every context of detraditionalisation offers the possibility of greater freedom of action than existed before. We are talking here about human emancipation from the constraints of the past. Addiction comes into play when choice, which should be driven by autonomy, is subverted by anxiety. In tradition, the past structures the present through shared collective beliefs and sentiments. The addict is also in thrall to the past – but because he or she cannot break away from what were originally freely chosen lifestyle habits.

As the influence of tradition and custom shrink on a world-wide level, the very basis of our self-identity – our sense of self – changes. In more traditional situations, a sense of self is sustained largely through the stability of the social positions of individuals in the community. Where tradition lapses, and lifestyle choice prevails, the self isn't exempt. Self-identity has to be created and recreated on a more active basis than before. This explains why therapy and counselling of all kinds have become so popular in Western countries. When he initiated modern psychoanalysis, Freud thought that he was establishing a scientific treatment for neurosis. What he was in effect doing was constructing a method for the renewal of self-identity, in the early stages of a detraditionalising culture.

After all, what happens in psychoanalysis is that the

individual revisits his or her past in order to create more autonomy for the future. Much the same is true in the self-help groups that have become so common in Western societies. At Alcoholics Anonymous meetings, for instance, individuals recount their life histories, and receive support from others present in stating their desire to change. They recover from their addiction essentially through rewriting the story-line of their lives.

The struggle between addiction and autonomy is at one pole of globalisation. At the other is the clash between a cosmopolitan outlook and fundamentalism. One might think that fundamentalism has always existed. This is not so – it has arisen in response to the globalising influences we see all round us. The term itself dates from the turn of the century, when it was used to refer to the beliefs of some Protestant sects in the US, particularly those who rejected Darwin. Yet even in the late 1950s there was no entry for the word 'fundamentalism' in the large Oxford English dictionary. It has come into common coinage only since the 1960s.

Fundamentalism is not the same as either fanaticism or authoritarianism. Fundamentalists call for a return to basic scriptures or texts, supposed to be read in a literal manner, and they propose that the doctrines derived from such a reading be applied to social, economic or political life. Fundamentalism gives new vitality and importance to the guardians of tradition. Only they have access to the 'exact meaning' of the texts. The clergy or other privileged interpreters gain secular as well as religious power. They may look to take over the reins of government directly – as happened in Iran – or work in conjunction with political parties.

Fundamentalism is a controversial word, because many of those called fundamentalists by others wouldn't accept the term as applying to themselves. So can an objective meaning be given to it? I think it can, and I would define it in the following fashion. Fundamentalism is beleaguered tradition. It is tradition defended in the traditional way – by reference to ritual truth – in a globalising world that asks for reasons. Fundamentalism, therefore, has nothing to do with the context of beliefs, religious or otherwise. What matters is how the truth of beliefs is defended or asserted.

Fundamentalism isn't about what people believe but, like tradition more generally, about why they believe it and how they justify it. It isn't confined to religion. The Chinese Red Guards, with their devotion to Mao's Little Red Book, were surely fundamentalists. Nor is fundamentalism primarily about the resistance of more traditional cultures to Westernisation – a rejection of Western decadence. Fundamentalism can develop on the soil of traditions of all sorts. It has no time for ambiguity, multiple interpretation or multiple identity – it is a refusal of dialogue in a world whose peace and continuity depend on it.

Fundamentalism is a child of globalisation, which it

both responds to and utilises. Fundamentalist groups almost everywhere have made extensive use of new communications technologies. Before he came to power in Iran, the Ayatollah Khomeini circulated videos and cassettes of his teachings. Hindutwa militants have made extensive use of the Internet and electronic mail to create a 'feeling of Hindu identity'.

Whatever form it takes – religious, ethnic, nationalist or directly political – I think it right to regard fundamentalism as problematic. It is edged with the possibility of violence, and it is the enemy of cosmopolitan values.

Yet fundamentalism isn't just the antithesis of globalising modernity, but poses questions to it. The most basic one is this: can we live in a world where nothing is sacred? I have to say, in conclusion, that I don't think we can. Cosmopolitans, of whom I count myself one, have to make plain that tolerance and dialogue can themselves be guided by values of a universal kind.

All of us need moral commitments that stand above the petty concerns and squabbles of everyday life. We should be prepared to mount an active defence of these values wherever they are poorly developed, or threatened. Cosmopolitan morality itself needs to be driven by passion. None of us would have anything to live for if we didn't have something worth dying for.

4

Family

Among all the changes going on in the world, none is more important than those happening in our personal lives – in sexuality, relationships, marriage and the family. There is a global revolution going on in how we think of ourselves and how we form ties and connections with others. It is a revolution advancing unevenly in different regions and cultures, with many resistances.

As with other aspects of the runaway world, we don't know quite what the ratio of advantages and problems will turn out to be. In some ways these are the most difficult and disturbing transformations of all. Most of us can tune out from larger problems for much of the time – one of the reasons it is difficult to work together to resolve them. We can't opt out, however, from the swirl of change reaching right into the heart of our emotional lives.

There are few countries in the world where there isn't intense discussion about sexual equality, the regulation of sexuality and the future of the family. And where there isn't open debate, this is mostly because it is actively repressed by authoritarian governments or fundamentalist groups. In many cases, these controversies are national or local – as are the social and political reactions to them. Politicians and pressure groups will suggest that if only family policy were modified, if only divorce were made harder or easier to get in their particular country, solutions to our problems could readily be found.

But the transformations affecting the personal and emotional spheres go far beyond the borders of any particular country, even one as large as the United States. We find parallel trends almost everywhere, varying only in degree and according to the cultural context in which they take place.

In China, for example, the state is considering making divorce more difficult. In the aftermath of the Cultural Revolution, very liberal marriage laws were passed. According to these laws, marriage is regarded as a working contract that can be dissolved 'when husband and wife both desire it'. Even if one partner objects, divorce can be granted when 'mutual affection' has gone from the marriage. Only a two week wait is required, after which the couple pay $4 and are henceforth independent. The Chinese divorce rate is still low as compared with Western countries, but it is rising rapidly – as is true in the other developing Asian societies. In Chinese cities, not only divorce but also cohabitation are becoming more frequent. In the vast Chinese countryside, by contrast, everything is different. Marriage and the family are much more traditional – in spite of the official policy of limiting childbirth through a mixture of incentives and punishment. Marriage is an arrangement between two families, fixed by the parents rather than the individuals concerned. A recent study in the province of Gansu, which has only a low level of economic development, found that 60 per cent of marriages are still arranged by parents. As a Chinese saying has it: 'Meet once, nod your head and marry'. There is a twist in the tail in modernising China. Many of those currently divorcing in the urban centres were originally married in the traditional manner in the country.

In China there is much talk of protecting the family. In many Western countries the debate is even more shrill. The family is a site for the struggles between tradition and modernity, but also a metaphor for them. There is perhaps more nostalgia surrounding the lost haven of the family than for any other institution with its roots in the past. Politicians and activists routinely diagnose the breakdown of family life and call for a return to the traditional family.

The 'traditional family' is very much a catch-all category. There have been many different types of family and kinship systems in different societies and cultures. The Chinese family, for instance, was always distinct from family forms in the West. Arranged marriage was never as common in most European countries, as in China or India. Yet the family in non-modern cultures did, and does, have some traits found more or less everywhere.

The traditional family was above all an economic unit. Agricultural production normally involved the whole family group, while among the gentry and aristocracy transmission of property was the main basis of marriage. In medieval Europe, marriage was not contracted on the basis of sexual love, nor was it regarded as a place where such love should flourish. As the French historian, Georges Duby, puts it, marriage in the Middle Ages was not to involve 'frivolity, passion, or fantasy'.

The inequality of men and women was intrinsic to the traditional family. I don't think one could overstate the importance of this. In Europe, women were the property of their husbands or fathers – chattels as defined in law. Inequality between men and women of course extended through to sexual life. The sexual double standard was directly bound up with the need to ensure continuity in lineage and inheritance. For most of history, men have made extensive, and sometimes quite conspicuous, use of mistresses, courtesans and prostitutes. The more affluent had amorous adventures with servants. But men needed to make sure that their wives were the mothers of their children. What was praised in respectable girls was virginity and, in wives, constancy and fidelity.

In the traditional family it wasn't only women who lacked rights: children did too. The idea of enshrining children's rights in law is in historical terms relatively recent. In premodern periods, as in traditional cultures today, children weren't reared for their own sake, or for the satisfaction of the parents. One could almost say that children weren't recognised as individuals. It wasn't that parents didn't love their children, but they cared about them more for the contribution they made to the common economic task than for themselves. Moreover, the death rate of children was frightening. In seventeenth-century Europe and America nearly one in four infants died in their first year. Almost 50 per cent didn't live to age ten.

Except for certain courtly or elite groups, in the traditional family sexuality was always dominated by reproduction. This was a matter of tradition and nature combined. The absence of effective contraception meant that for most women sexuality was inevitably closely connected with childbirth. In many traditional cultures, including in Western Europe up to the threshold of the twentieth century, a woman might have ten or more pregnancies during the course of her life.

For reasons already given, sexuality was dominated by the idea of female virtue. The sexual double standard is often thought of as a creation of Victorian Britain. In fact, in one version or another it was central to all non-modern societies. It involved a dualistic view of female sexuality – a clear-cut division between the virtuous woman on the one hand and the libertine on the other. Sexual adventurism in many cultures has been taken as a positive defining feature of masculinity. James Bond is, or was, admired for his sexual as well as his physical heroism. Sexually adventurous women, by contrast, have nearly always been beyond the pale, no matter how much influence the mistresses of some prominent figures might have achieved.

Attitudes towards homosexuality were also governed by a mix of tradition and nature. Anthropological surveys show that homosexuality – or male homosexuality at any rate – has been tolerated, or openly approved of, in more cultures than it has been proscribed. For example, in some societies young boys were encouraged to establish homosexual relationships with older men as a form of sexual tutelage. Such activities were expected to stop when the youths got engaged or married. Those societies that have been hostile to homosexuality have ordinarily condemned it as specifically unnatural. Western attitudes have been more extreme than most; less than half a century ago homosexuality was still widely regarded as a perversion and written up as such in manuals of psychiatry.

Of course, antagonism towards homosexuality is still widespread and the dualistic view of women continues to be held by many – men and women alike. Nevertheless, over the past few decades the main elements of our sexual lives in the West have changed in an absolutely basic way. The separation of sexuality from reproduction is in principle complete. Sexuality is for the first time something to be discovered, moulded, altered. Sexuality, which used to be defined so strictly in relation to marriage and legitimacy, now has little connection to them at all. We should see the increasing acceptance of homosexuality not just as a tribute to liberal tolerance. It is a logical outcome of the severance of sexuality from reproduction. Sexuality which has no content is by definition no longer dominated by heterosexuality.

What most of its defenders in Western countries call the traditional family was in fact a late, transitional phase in family development in the 1950s. This was a time at which the proportion of women out at work was still relatively low and when it was still difficult, especially for women, to obtain divorce without stigma. However, men and women by this time were more equal than they had been previously, both in fact and in law. The family had ceased to be an economic entity and the idea of romantic love as a basis for marriage had replaced marriage as an economic contract. Since then, the family has changed much further.

The details vary from society to society, but the same

trends are visible almost everywhere in the industrialised world. Only a minority of people now live in what might be called the standard 1950s family – both parents living together with their children of the marriage, where the mother is a full-time housewife and the father the breadwinner. In some countries, more than a third of all births happen outside wedlock, while the proportion of people living alone has gone up steeply and looks likely to rise even more. In most societies, like the US or Britain, marriage remains very popular – these have aptly been called high divorce, high marriage societies. In Scandinavia, on the other hand, a large proportion of people living together, including where children are involved, remain unmarried. Up to a quarter of women aged between 18 and 35 in the United States and Europe say they do not intend to have children – and they appear to mean it.

In all countries a diversity of family forms continues to exist. In the US, many people, recent immigrants particularly, still live according to traditional values. Most family life, however, has been transformed by the rise of the *couple* and coupledom. Marriage and the family have become what I termed in Chapter 1 shell institutions: they are still called the same, but inside their basic character has changed. In the traditional family, the married couple was only one part, and often not the main part, of the family system. Ties with children and with other relatives tended to be equally or even more important in the day-to-day conduct of social life. Today the couple, married or unmarried, is at the core of what the family is. The couple came to be at the centre of family life as the economic role of the family dwindled and love, or love plus sexual attraction, became the basis of forming marriage ties.

A couple once constituted has its own exclusive history, its own biography. It is a unit based upon emotional communication or intimacy. The idea of intimacy, like so many other familiar notions I've discussed in this book, sounds old but in fact is very new. Marriage was never in the past based upon intimacy – emotional communication. No doubt this was important to a good marriage but it was not the foundation of it. For the couple, it is. Communication is the means of establishing the tie in the first place and it is the chief rationale for its continuation.

We should recognise what a major transition this is. 'Coupling' and 'uncoupling' provide a more accurate description of the arena of personal life now than do 'marriage and the family'. A more important question for us than 'Are you married?' is 'Are you in a relationship?' The idea of a relationship is also surprisingly recent. In the 1960s no one spoke of 'relationships'. They didn't need to, nor did they need to speak in terms of intimacy and commitment. Marriage at that time *was* the commitment, as the existence of shotgun marriages bore witness.

In the traditional family, marriage was a bit like a state of nature. Both for men and for women it was defined as a stage of life that the large majority was expected to go through. Those who remained outside were regarded with some scorn or condescension – particularly the spinster, but the bachelor too if he held out for too long.

While statistically marriage is still the normal condition, for most people the meaning of marriage has more or less completely changed. Marriage signifies that a couple is in a stable relationship, and may indeed promote that stability, since it makes a public declaration of commitment. However, marriage is no longer the chief defining basis of coupledom.

The position of children in all this is interesting and somewhat paradoxical. Our attitudes towards children and their protection have altered radically over the past several generations. We prize children so much partly because they have become so much rarer, and partly because the decision to have a child is very different from what it was for previous generations. In the traditional family, children were an economic benefit. Today in Western countries a child, on the contrary, puts a large financial burden on the parents. Having a child is more of a distinct and specific decision than it used to be, and it is a decision guided by psychological and emotional needs. The worries we have about the effects of divorce upon children, and the existence of many fatherless families, have to be understood against the background of our much higher expectations about how children should be cared for and protected.

There are three main areas in which emotional communication, and therefore intimacy, are replacing the old ties that used to bind together people's personal lives – in sexual and love relationships, parent–child relationships and also in friendship.

To analyse these I want to use the idea of the 'pure relationship'. I mean by this a relationship based upon emotional communication, where the rewards derived from such communication are the main basis for the relationship to continue. I don't mean a sexually pure relationship. Also I don't mean anything that exists in reality. I'm talking of an abstract idea that helps us understand changes going on in the world. Each of the three areas just mentioned – sexual and love relationships, parent–child relationships and friendship – is tending to approximate to this model. Emotional communication or intimacy is becoming the key to what they are all about.

The pure relationship has quite different dynamics from more traditional kinds of social ties. It depends upon processes of active trust – opening oneself up to the other. Disclosure is the basic condition of intimacy. The pure relationship is implicitly democratic. When I was originally working on the study of intimate relationships, I read a great deal of therapeutic and self-help literature on the subject. I was struck by something that

I don't believe has been widely noticed or remarked upon. If one looks at how a therapist sees a good relationship – in any of the three spheres just mentioned – it is striking how direct a parallel there is with public democracy.

A good relationship, it goes without saying, is an ideal – most ordinary relationships don't come even close. I'm not suggesting that our relations with spouses, lovers, children or friends aren't often messy, conflictful and unsatisfying. But the principles of democracy are ideals too, that also often stand at some large distance from reality.

A good relationship is a relationship of equals, where each party has equal rights and obligations. In such a relationship, each person has respect, and wants the best for the other. The pure relationship is based upon communication, so that understanding the other person's point of view is essential. Talk, or dialogue, is the basis of making the relationship work. Relationships function best if people don't hide too much from each other – there has to be mutual trust. And trust has to be worked at; it can't just be taken for granted. Finally, a good relationship is one free from arbitrary power, coercion or violence.

Every one of these qualities conforms to the values of democratic politics. In a democracy, all are in principle equal, and with equality of rights and responsibilities – as a matter of principle, at any rate – comes mutual respect. Open dialogue is a core property of democracy. Democratic systems seek to substitute open discussion of issues – a public space of dialogue – for authoritarian power, or for the sedimented power of tradition. No democracy can work without trust. And democracy is undermined if it gives way to authoritarianism or violence.

When we apply these principles – as ideals – to relationships, we are talking of something very important – the possible emergence of what I shall call a democracy of the emotions in everyday life. A democracy of the emotions, it seems to me, is just as important as public democracy in improving the quality of our lives.

This applies as much in parent–child relationships as in other areas. These can't, and shouldn't, be materially equal. Parents must have authority over children, in everyone's interests. Yet they should presume an in principle equality. In a democratic family, the authority of parents should be based upon an implicit contract. The parent in effect says to the child: 'If you were an adult, and knew what I know, you would agree that what I ask you to do is good for you'. Children in traditional families were – and are – supposed to be seen and not heard. Many parents, perhaps despairing of their children's rebelliousness, would dearly like to resurrect that rule. But there isn't any going back to it, nor should there be. In a democracy of the emotions, children can and should be able to answer back.

A democracy of the emotions doesn't imply lack of discipline or absence of respect. It simply seeks to put them on a different footing. Something very similar happened in the public sphere when democracy began to replace arbitrary government and the rule of force.

A democracy of the emotions would draw no distinctions of principle between heterosexual and same-sex relationships. Gays rather than heterosexuals have been pioneers in discovering the new world of relationships and exploring its possibilities. They have had to be, because when homosexuality came out of the closet, gays weren't able to depend upon the normal supports of traditional marriage.

To speak of fostering an emotional democracy does not mean being weak about family duties, or about public policy towards the family. Democracy means the acceptance of obligations, as well as rights sanctioned in law. The protection of children has to be the primary feature of legislation and public policy. Parents should be legally obliged to provide for their children until adulthood, no matter what living arrangements they enter into. Marriage is no longer an economic institution, yet as a ritual commitment it can help stabilise otherwise fragile relationships. If this applies to heterosexual relationships, it must apply to homosexual ones too.

There are many questions to be asked of all this – too many to answer in a short chapter. The most obvious is that I have concentrated mainly upon trends affecting the family in Western countries. What about areas where the traditional family remains largely intact, as in the example of China with which I began? Will the changes observed in the West become more and more global?

I think they will – indeed that they are. It isn't a question of *whether* existing forms of traditional family will become modified, but when and how. I would venture even further. What I have described as an emerging democracy of the emotions is on the front line in the struggle between cosmopolitanism and fundamentalism that I described previously. Equality of the sexes, and the sexual freedom of women, which are incompatible with the traditional family, are anathema to fundamentalist groups. Opposition to them, indeed, is one of the defining features of religious fundamentalism across the world.

There is plenty to be worried about in the state of the family, in Western countries and elsewhere. It is just as mistaken to say that every family form is as good as any other, as to argue that the decline of the traditional family is a disaster. I would turn the argument of the political and fundamentalist right on its head. The persistence of the traditional family – or aspects of it – in many parts of the world is more worrisome than its decline. For what are the most important forces promoting democracy and economic development in poorer countries? Well, precisely the equality and education of women. And what must be changed to make this possible? Most importantly, the traditional family.

Sexual equality is not just a core principle of democracy. It is also relevant to happiness and fulfilment. Many of the changes happening to the family are problematic and difficult. But surveys in the US and Europe show that few want to go back to traditional male and female roles, or to legally defined inequality. If ever I am tempted to think that the traditional family might be best after all, I remember what my great aunt once said to me. She must have had one of the longest marriages of anyone, having been with her husband for over 60 years. She once confided that she had been deeply unhappy with him the whole of that time. In her day there was no escape.

5

Democracy

On 9 November 1989, I was in Berlin, in what was then West Germany. At the meeting I had come to take part in, some of those present were from East Berlin. One such person, who was away that afternoon, later came back in a state of some excitement. He had been in the East, and was told that the Berlin Wall was on the point of being opened.

A small group of us got down there very quickly. Ladders were being put against it and we started to climb up. But we were pushed back by television crews who had just arrived on the scene. They had to go up first, they said, so that they could film us scaling the ladders and arriving at the top. They even persuaded some people to go back down and climb up twice, to make sure they had good television footage.

Thus is history made in the closing years of the twentieth century. Television not only gets there first, but also stages the spectacle. In a way, as I shall go on to argue, the television crews had the right to push themselves to the front. For television had an important role in making the opening of the Wall happen, as it did more generally in the transformations of 1989 in Eastern Europe. The driving force of the 1989 revolutions was democracy or self-rule. And the spread of democracy, I shall try to show, has been strongly influenced in the recent period by the advance of global communications.

Democracy is perhaps the most powerful energising idea of the twentieth century. There are few states in the world today that don't call themselves democratic. The former Soviet Union and its East European dependencies labelled themselves 'people's democracies', as communist China continues to do. Virtually the only countries that are explicitly non-democratic are the last remaining semi-feudal monarchies, such as Saudi Arabia – and even these are hardly untouched by democratic currents.

What is democracy? The issue is a contentious one, and many different interpretations have been offered. I shall mean by it the following. Democracy is a system involving effective competition between political parties for positions of power. In a democracy, there are regular and fair elections, in which all members of the population may take part. These rights of democratic participation go along with civil liberties – freedom of expression and discussion, together with the freedom to form and join political groups or associations.

Democracy isn't an all or nothing thing. There can be different forms, as well as different levels, of democratisation. Democracy in Britain and the United States, for instance, has contrasting qualities. A British traveller in the US once enquired of an American companion: 'How can you bear to be governed by people you wouldn't dream of inviting to dinner?', to which the American replied, 'How can you bear to be governed by people who wouldn't dream of inviting you to dinner?'

Everyone is a democrat now, but it certainly wasn't always so. Democratic ideas were fiercely resisted by established elites and ruling groups in the nineteenth century, and often treated with derision. Democracy was the inspiring ideal of the American and French revolutions, but for a long while its hold was limited. Only a minority of the population had the vote. Even some of the most fervent advocates of democratic government, such as the political philosopher John Stuart Mill, argued that limitations should be imposed on it. Mill recommended that some of the electorate should have more votes than others, so that in his words, the 'wiser and talented' have more influence than the 'ignorant and less able'.

Democracy in the West became fully developed only in the twentieth century. Before the First World War, women had the vote in only four countries – Finland, Norway, Australia and New Zealand. Women didn't get the vote in Switzerland until as late as 1974. Moreover, some countries that became fully democratic later experienced relapses. Germany, Italy, Austria, Spain and Portugal all had periods of authoritarian rule or military dictatorship during the period from the 1930s to the 1970s. Outside Europe, North America and Australasia, there have been only a small number of long-standing democracies, such as Costa Rica in Latin America.

Over the past few decades, however, much of this has changed, and in a remarkable way. Since the mid-1970s, the number of democratic governments in the world has more than doubled. Democracy has spread to over 30 more countries, while all the existing democratic states have kept democratic institutions in place. These changes began in Mediterranean Europe, with the overthrow of the military regimes in Greece, Spain and Portugal. The second group of countries where democracy spread, this time mainly in the early 1980s, was in South and Central America. Some 12 countries established or re-established democratic government, including Brazil and Argentina.

The story continues across all continents. The transition to democracy post-1989 in Eastern Europe, and parts of the former Soviet Union, was followed in a number of countries in Africa. In Asia, with some problems and reversals, democratisation has been going on over the whole period since the early 1970s – in countries such as South Korea, Taiwan, the Philippines, Bangladesh, Thailand and Mongolia. India has remained a democratic state since its independence in 1947.

Of course, some states making the passage to democracy fall short of full democratisation, or appear to have stalled along the way. Russia is only one of many examples. Others are simply putting back what existed before. Argentina, and some other Latin American countries, have had democratic government previously, as have the Czech Republic, or Poland in Eastern Europe. Since democratic governments have often been overthrown, we can't be sure how permanent any of these democratic transitions will be. Yet democracy has made nearly as much advance since the 1960s as it did over more than a whole century before that. Why?

One possible answer is offered by those who take a triumphalist view of the Western combination of democracy and free markets. This is that other systems have been tried and have failed. Democracy has come out top because it is best. It simply took most countries outside the Western ambit some while to recognise this.

I wouldn't dispute part of the argument. Democracy *is* best. But as an account of the recent waves of democratisation, it is hardly adequate. It doesn't explain why such changes should happen at this juncture in history.

To get a better explanation, we need to resolve what I shall call the paradox of democracy. The paradox of democracy is that democracy is spreading over the world, as I have just described, yet in the mature democracies, which the rest of the world is supposed to be copying, there is widespread disillusionment with democratic processes. In most Western countries, levels of trust in politicians have dropped over past years. Fewer people turn out to vote than used to, particularly in the US. More and more people say that they are uninterested in parliamentary politics, especially among the younger generation. Why are citizens in democratic countries apparently becoming disillusioned with democratic government, at the same time as it is spreading round the rest of the world?

The changes that I have been analysing throughout this book explain why. For increasing numbers across the world, life is no longer lived as fate – as relatively fixed and determined. Authoritarian government becomes out of line with other life experiences, including the flexibility and dynamism necessary to compete in the global electronic economy. Political power based upon authoritarian command can no longer draw upon reserves of traditional deference, or respect.

In a world based upon active communication, hard power – power that comes only from the top down – loses its edge. The economic conditions that the top-down Soviet economy, or other authoritarian regimes, couldn't handle – the need for decentralisation and flexibility – were mirrored in politics. Information monopoly, upon which the political system was based, has no future in an intrinsically open framework of global communications.

In the East European events of 1989, large numbers of people took to the streets. But – unlike almost any other revolution in history – there was remarkably little violence. What seemed a system of implacable power – communist totalitarianism – faded away as though it had hardly existed. Few thought apartheid in South Africa could disappear without being forcibly overthrown. But it did.

The only episodes of violence that occurred in 1989 were involved in the seizure of television stations. Those who invaded them got their priorities right. The communications revolution has produced more active, reflexive citizenries than existed before. It is these very developments that are at the same time producing disaffection in the long-established democracies. In a detraditionalising world, politicians can't rely upon the old forms of pomp and circumstance to justify what they do. Orthodox parliamentary politics becomes remote from the flood of change sweeping through people's lives.

Where does this leave democracy itself? Should we accept that democratic institutions are becoming marginal just at the point where democracy seems on a roll?

Some very interesting findings are revealed in the opinion polls carried out in different Western countries

73

about trust in government. People have in fact lost a good deal of the trust they used to have in politicians and orthodox democratic procedures. They haven't lost their faith, however, in democratic processes. In a recent survey in the US and the major West European countries, well over 90 per cent of the population said that they approved of democratic government. Moreover, contrary to what many assume, most people aren't becoming disinterested in politics as such. The findings actually show the reverse. People are actually more interested in politics than they used to be. This includes the younger generation. Younger people are not, as has so often been said, a generation X, disaffected and alienated.

What they are, or many of them are, is more cynical about the claims that politicians make for themselves and – crucially – concerned about political questions about which they feel politicians have little to say. Many regard politics as a corrupt business, in which political leaders are self-interested rather than having the interests of their citizens at heart. Younger people see as most important issues such as ecological questions, human rights, family policy and sexual freedom. On an economic level, they don't believe that politicians are able to deal with the forces moving the world. As everyone understands, many of these go beyond the level of the nation-state. It isn't surprising that activists should choose to put their energies into special-interest groups, since these promise what orthodox politics seems unable to deliver.

How can democracy and active government be sustained when they seem to have lost their purchase on events? I think there is an answer. What is needed in the democratic countries is a deepening of democracy itself. I shall call this *democratising democracy*. But democracy today must also become transnational. We need to democratise above – as well as below – the level of the nation. A globalising era demands global responses, and this applies to politics just as much as any other area.

A deepening of democracy is required, because the old mechanisms of government don't work in a society where citizens live in the same information environment as those in power over them. Western democratic governments, of course, have never been as secretive as communist states or other types of authoritarian government. Yet secretive in some contexts they certainly have been. Think, for example, of how much was concealed by the US and British governments in the Cold War period about nuclear testing and weapons development. Western democratic systems have also involved old boy networks, political patronage and backstage deals. They frequently make use of traditional symbolism, and traditional forms of power, that are less than wholly democratic. The House of Lords in the UK is only one of the most obvious of such examples. As traditions lose their grip, what once seemed venerable, and worthy of respect, almost overnight can come to appear quaint, or even ridiculous.

It is not by accident that there have been so many corruption scandals in politics around the world in the past few years. From Japan to Germany, France and the US to the UK, corruption cases have made the news. I doubt that corruption is more common in democratic countries than it used to be. Rather, in an open information society it is more visible, and the boundaries of what counts as corruption have shifted. In Britain, for example, the old boy network in the past was simply the way things were done, even when left-of-centre parties were in power. Such networks have hardly disappeared, but much of what used to happen through them, and be widely accepted, is now defined as illegitimate.

The democratising of democracy will take different forms in different countries, depending on their background. But there isn't any country so advanced that it is exempt. Democratising democracy means having an effective devolution of power, where – as in Britain – it is still strongly concentrated at the national level. It means having effective anti-corruption measures at all levels.

It often also implies constitutional reform, and the promotion of greater transparency in political affairs. We should also be prepared to experiment with alternative democratic procedures, especially when these might help bring political decision making close to the everyday concerns of citizens. People's juries, for example, or electronic referenda won't replace representative democracy, but they can be a useful complement to it.

Political parties will have to get more used to collaborating with single-issue groups, such as ecological pressure groups, than they have in the past. Some people see contemporary societies as fragmented and disorganised, but in fact the opposite is true. People are getting more involved in groups and associations than they used to. In Britain, 20 times more people belong to voluntary or self-help groups than are members of political parties, and much the same is true of other countries.

Single-issue groups are often at the forefront in raising problems and questions that may go ignored in orthodox political circles until too late. Thus well before the BSE crisis in the UK, groups and movements had been warning about the dangers of contamination in the food chain.

The democratising of democracy also depends upon the fostering of a strong civic culture. Markets cannot produce such a culture. Nor can a pluralism of special-interest groups. We shouldn't think of there being only two sectors of society, the state and the market-place – or the public and private. In between is the area of civil society, including the family and other non-economic institutions. Building a democracy of the emotions is one part of a progressive civic culture. Civil society is the arena in which democratic attitudes, including tolerance, have to be developed. The civic sphere can be fostered by government, but is in turn its cultural basis.

The democratising of democracy isn't relevant only to the mature democracies. It can help build democratic institutions where they are weak and undernourished. In Russia, for instance, where gangster capitalism is rife and strong authoritarian overtones persist from the past, a more open and democratic society can't be built only in a top–down manner. It has to be constructed bottom up, through the revival of civic culture. Replacing state control with markets, even if they were more stable than they are, wouldn't achieve this end. A well-functioning democracy has been aptly compared to a three-legged stool. Government, the economy and civil society need to be in balance. If one dominates over the others, unfortunate consequences follow. In the former Soviet Union, the state dominated most areas of life. Hence, there wasn't an energetic economy and civil society was all but killed off.

We can't leave the media out of this equation. The media, particularly television, have a double relation to democracy. On the one hand, as I have stressed, the emergence of a global information society is a powerful democratising force. On the other hand, television and the other media tend to destroy the very public space of dialogue they open up, through a relentless trivialising, and personalising, of political issues. Moreover, the growth of giant multinational media corporations means that unelected business tycoons can hold enormous power.

Countering such power can't be a matter of national policy alone. Crucially, the democratising of democracy can't stop at the level of the nation-state. As practised up to now, democratic politics has presumed a national community that is self-governing and able to shape most of the policies that concern it. It has presumed the sovereign nation. But under the impact of globalisation, sovereignty has become fuzzy. Nations and nation-states remain powerful, but there are large democratic deficits opening up – as the political scientist, David Held, points out – between them and the global forces that affect the lives of their citizens. Ecological risks, fluctuations in the global economy, or global technological change, do not respect the borders of nations. They escape democratic processes – one of the main reasons, as I said earlier, for the declining appeal of democracy where it is best established.

Talk of democracy above the level of the nation might seem quite unrealistic. Such ideas, after all, were widely spoken of a hundred years ago. Instead of an era of global harmony, there arrived the two world wars; more than a hundred million people have been killed in warfare during the twentieth century.

Are circumstances different now? Obviously no one can say for sure, but I believe they are. I have given the reasons in earlier chapters. The world is much more interdependent than it was a century ago, and the nature of world society has changed. As a reverse side of the coin, the shared problems we face today – such as global ecological risks – are also much greater.

How might democracy be fostered above the level of the nation-state? I would look to the transnational organisations as much as the international ones. The United Nations, as its very name indicates, is an association of nation-states. For the moment at least, it rarely challenges the sovereignty of nations, and indeed its charter asserts that it should not do so. The European Union is different. I would see it as forging a way that could, and very likely will, be followed in other regions too. What is important about the EU isn't that it is located in Europe, but that it is pioneering a form of transnational governance. Contrary to what some of its supporters and its critics say, it is not a federal state or a super nation-state. But nor is it merely an association of nations. The countries which have entered the EU have voluntarily given up some of their sovereignty in order to do so.

Now, the European Union isn't itself particularly democratic. It has famously been said of the EU that if it applied to join itself, it wouldn't get in. The EU doesn't meet the democratic criteria it demands of its members. Yet there is nothing in principle that prevents its further democratisation and we should press hard for such change.

The existence of the EU drives home a cardinal principle of democracy, when seen against the background of the global order. This is that the transnational system can actively contribute to democracy within states, as well as between them. The European courts, for example, have made a range of decisions, including measures protecting individual rights, that hold within the member countries.

As we look round the globe at the end of the twentieth century, we can see cause for optimism and pessimism in about equal measure. The expansion of democracy is a case in point. On the face of it, democracy seems a fragile flower. In spite of its spread, oppressive regimes abound, while human rights are routinely flouted in states around the world. In Kosovo, hundreds of thousands were forced from their homes, and all pretence of the rule of law abandoned. I would like to quote some words here, from a reporter who observed the events: 'Nearly half a million refugees', he wrote, 'are in Macedonia. How they are to be fed, nobody knows … Come over into Macedonia and help us!' This was published in the *Toronto Daily Star*. The reporter was Ernest Hemingway, the date 20 October 1922.

One might be forgiven for thinking that some problems are simply intractable, without hope of resolution. Democracy might appear to flourish only in especially fertile soil, which has been cultivated in the long term. In societies, or regions, that have little history of democratic government, democracy seems to have shallow roots and is easily swept away. Yet perhaps all this is changing. Rather than thinking of democracy as a fragile flower, easily trampled underfoot, perhaps we should see it more as a sturdy plant, able to grow even on quite barren ground. If my argument is correct, the expansion of democracy is bound up with structural changes in world society. Nothing comes without struggle. But the furthering of democracy at all levels is worth fighting for and it can be achieved. Our runaway world doesn't need less, but more government – and this, only democratic institutions can provide.

Selected reading

Globalisation

Albrow, Martin. *The Global Age: State and Society Beyond Modernity*. Cambridge: Polity Press, 1996.
The author states that we are entering the first global age. Rather than talking about globalisation, we should be analysing the ways in which living in the global age draws us all into new forms of interdependence.

Bell, Daniel. 'The world and the United States in 2013'. *Daedalus*, 116(3), 1987, 1–31.
This article is an attempt at predicting the major structural changes of the future. It comes to the conclusion that there is a mismatch of scale between globalising forces and the institutions of the modern nation-state.

Castells, Manuel. *The Rise of the Network Society (The Information Age*, vol. 1). Cambridge, MA: Blackwell, 1996.
The first volume of a three volume study on the rise of

the 'network society' – a global order formed by the emergence of the role of information in the new global economy.

Dicken, Peter. *Global Shift: Transforming the World Economy*, 3rd edn. London: Chapman, 1998.
A revised and updated account of the changing patterns of global economic activity. It presents evidence from different industry sectors and addresses the question of how economic globalisation affects national sovereignty.

Gray, John. *False Dawn: The Delusions of Global Capitalism*. London: Granta Books, 1998.
A very forceful work, arguing that the expansion of the global market-place is producing numerous social problems across the world. The author says that there cannot be one model of capitalist development that can apply to all countries and all areas.

Held, David, Anthony McGrew, David Goldblatt and Jonathan Perraton. *Global Transformations: Politics, Economics and Culture*. Cambridge: Polity Press, 1999.
The most comprehensive introduction to the subject of globalisation produced to date, with a very balanced analysis of different views. It introduced the division between 'globalisation sceptics' and others that I make use of in the opening chapter.

Hirst, Paul Q., and Grahame Thompson. *Globalization in Question: The International Economy and the Possibilities of Governance*. Cambridge: Polity Press, 1996.
Hirst and Thompson take a sceptical view of globalisation, arguing that the degree of economic integration in world markets has often been greatly overestimated.

Korten, David C. *When Corporations Rule the World*. West Hartford, CN and San Francisco, CA: Kumarian Press and Berrett-Koehler, 1995.
A study of the development of global economic power, concentrating upon the role played by the giant corporations. The author argues that adequate changes need to be made to confine this power.

McLuhan, Marshall. *The Gutenberg Galaxy: The Making of Typographic Man*. Toronto: University of Toronto Press, 1962.
Introduced the often quoted term of a 'global village' in order to grasp the impact of new communication technologies on our lives.

Ohmae, Kenichi. *The End of the Nation State: The Rise of Regional Economies*. London: HarperCollins, 1995.
Ohmae takes something of an opposite view from Hirst and Thompson, proposing that the advance of globalisation has been so strong that nation-states have

lost most of their power to control their own affairs.

Soros, George. *The Crisis of Global Capitalism: Open Society Endangered*. New York: BBS/Public Affairs, 1998.
George Soros is one of the most successful financiers of recent years. He has made a fortune from the financial markets, but believes that they need greater regulation than at present. Otherwise there would be more crises like that affecting the East Asian economies in 1998.

Strange, Susan. *The Retreat of the State: the Diffusion of Power in the World Economy*. Cambridge: Cambridge University Press, 1996.
Written by the author of *Casino Capitalism* (Oxford: Blackwell, 1986), this book argues that the emergence of transnational economic and political organisations has led to an important power shift in the international political economy.

Risk

Adams, John. *Risk*. London: UCL Press, 1994.
An interesting discussion of the nature of risk and risk management. Adams argues that the analysis of risk must take account of how people selectively respond to perceived risk in their own behaviour.

Beck, Ulrich. *Risk Society: Towards a New Modernity.* London: Sage, 1992.
A classic book which argues that we are moving from an 'industrial society' to a 'risk society'. A risk society is one marked by new uncertainties, by rising individualism and by basic changes in major social institutions.

Beck, Ulrich. *Ecological Politics in an Age of Risk.* Cambridge: Polity Press, 1995.
Relates the rise of ecological politics to the transformation of nature by modern technology. We start to become concerned about 'nature' in a world only where very little is any more 'natural'.

Bernstein, Peter L. *Against the Gods: The Remarkable Story of Risk.* New York: John Wiley & Sons, 1996.
The best discussion of risk in relation to the history of probability theory and the development of financial markets. Bernstein shows how more and more sophisticated forms of risk assessment have developed over the centuries.

Douglas, Mary, and Aaron Wildavsky. *Risk and Culture: an Essay on the Selection of Technical and Environmental Dangers.* Berkeley, CA: University of California Press, 1982.
The authors argue that risk cannot be defined

objectively. What counts as 'risk' depends upon the values held by individuals or groups.

Franklin, Jane (ed.). *The Politics of Risk Society.*
Cambridge: Polity Press, 1998.
A collection of articles discussing different aspects of risk in contemporary societies.

Knight, Frank Hyneman. *Risk, Uncertainty and Profit.*
Boston, MA: Houghton Mifflin, 1921.
In this classic text, the author applies the concept of risk to economic activity and develops a distinction between 'risk' and 'uncertainty'. Many have been influenced by this distinction, which is that risk can be calculated, whereas uncertainty cannot.

Raphael, Adam. *Ultimate Risk.* London: Bantam Press, 1994.
An interesting account of the various problems faced by Lloyd's Insurance Company. The author argues that the troubles at Lloyd's in London stemmed from major deficiencies in risk management.

Royal Society. *Risk: Analysis, Perception, Management.*
London: Royal Society, 1992.
An 'official' account of risk produced by the most respectable scientific body in the UK. Generated considerable dispute about 'objective' versus 'subjective' risk.

Tradition

Ahmed, Akbar S., and Hastings Donnan (eds). *Islam, Globalization, and Postmodernity*. London and New York: Routledge, 1994.
Shows the connections between the rise of fundamentalism and the expansion of the mass media. Fundamentalism is not a national, but a transnational phenomenon.

Gellner, Ernest. *Postmodernism, Reason and Religion*. New York: Routledge, 1992.
A provocative discussion of the resurgence and significance of religion in current time. Religious traditions don't just die but are being continually revived.

Gross, David. *The Past in Ruins: Tradition and the Critique of Modernity*. Amherst, MA: University of Massachusetts Press, 1992.
An interpretation of the changing character of tradition against the backdrop of cultural theory.

Heelas, Paul, Scott Lash and Paul Morris (eds). *Detraditionalization: Critical Reflections on Authority and Identity*. Oxford: Blackwell, 1996.
A collection of articles discussing the decline of tradition in contemporary societies. Different

viewpoints are expressed about how far such a decline has actually occurred and what its implications might be.

Hobsbawm, Eric J., and Terrence O. Ranger. *The Invention of Tradition.* Cambridge: Cambridge University Press, 1983.
A classic work showing that many forms of behaviour that we tend to assume come from time immemorial are actually recently constructed.

Huntington, Samuel P. *The Clash of Civilizations and the Remaking of World Order.* New York: Simon & Schuster, 1996.
A now famous study of new divisions in the world community arising in the post-1989 era. Huntington argues that the new sources of conflict in the world centre upon the ancient fault lines between the different religious civilisations.

Kepel, Gilles. *The Revenge of God: The Resurgence of Islam, Christianity and Judaism in the Modern World.* Cambridge: Polity Press, 1994.
An excellent and interesting study of the rise of fundamentalism. The book concentrates particularly upon the complexities of applying the idea of 'fundamentalism' to Islam.

Kramnick, Isaac (ed.). *The Portable Enlightenment Reader.*
New York: Penguin, 1995.
A selection of works by the leading thinkers of the
eighteenth-century Enlightenment. Includes writings
by the Baron d'Holbach.

Marty, Martin E., and R. Scott Appleby (eds).
Fundamentalism Observed (*The Fundamentalism Project,*
vol. 1). Chicago: University of Chicago Press, 1991.
First of a multivolume study of the nature of
fundamentalism in the contemporary world.

Said, Edward W. *Orientalism.* London: Routledge &
Kegan Paul, 1979.
In this influential work, the author attacks our images
of other cultures and traditions. Rather than being
accurate descriptions, they often reflect an elevated
self-image of Western culture.

Shils, Edward A. *Tradition.* London: Faber & Faber,
1981.
A general discussion of the nature of tradition in
different societies and cultures. The author argues for a
positive view of tradition as essential to social
continuity and cohesion.

Vidal, Denis. 'When the gods drink milk: empiricism
and belief in contemporary Hinduism'. *South Asia*

Research, 18, 1998.
A study of the extraordinary episode that happened in India in 1995, when the images of the elephant-headed god, Ganesh, and other deities appeared to 'really' drink milk that was offered to them.

Family

Burgess, Adrienne. *Fatherhood Reclaimed: The Making of the Modern Father*. London: Vermilion, 1997.
Provides an account of the changing character of fatherhood in modern societies. The author argues that increasing attention should be given to fathers' rights.

Coontz, Stephanie. *The Way We Never Were: American Families and the Nostalgia Trap*. New York: Basic Books, 1992.
A masterful critique of nostalgia about past forms of family life. Coontz shows that there never was a 'golden age' of the family.

Duby, Georges. *Love and Marriage in the Middle Ages*. Cambridge: Polity Press, 1994.
A classic study of marriage, love and sexuality in the Middle Ages, showing how different many key attitudes were from now.

Foucault, Michel. *The History of Sexuality*, vol. 1. Harmondsworth: Penguin, 1981 (first published in 1976).
A celebrated discussion of the rise of Western preoccupation with sexuality. Focault argues that sexuality wasn't simply repressed in the Victorian era. Rather, the Victorians helped initiate our fascination with sex.

Goode, William J. *World Revolution and Family Patterns*. New York and London: Free Press and Collier-Macmillan, 1963.
A classic study of changes happening in the family world-wide. The author argues that there are common patterns of change found in many different countries and regions of the world.

Jamieson, Lynn. *Intimacy: Personal Relationships in Modern Societies*. Cambridge: Polity Press, 1998.
The author addresses the question of how intimate relationships have changed in modern society, drawing on empirical evidence from a range of Western countries.

Laslett, Peter. *The World We Have Lost*. London: Methuen, 1965.
A classic account of family life in past generations, questioning many myths about the family.

McLanahan, Sara S., and Gary D. Sandefur. *Growing Up with a Single Parent: What Hurts, What Helps*. Cambridge, MA: Harvard University Press, 1994.
The best study of the social and educational impact of single-parent families in the US.

Phillips, Roderick. *Untying the Knot: A Short History of Divorce*. Cambridge: Cambridge University Press, 1991.
A readable study of the history of divorce in Europe and the US.

Phoenix, Ann. *Young Mothers?* Oxford: Polity Press, 1990.
A discussion of the problems of teenage mothers in modern society.

Weeks, Jeffrey. *Sexuality*. Chichester: Ellis Horwood, 1986.
A lively and thorough introduction to the study of sexuality. The author provides a balanced account of different controversies about the nature of sexuality.

Democracy

Barber, Benjamin R. *A Place for Us: How to Make Society Civil and Democracy Strong*. New York: Hill and Wang, 1998.

A discussion of the relationship between democracy, civil society and corporate power. The author argues that effective democracy needs the regulation both of government and business, together with a secure foundation in the civil order.

Czempiel, Ernst O., and James N. Rosenau (eds). *Governance Without Government: Order and Change in World Politics.* Cambridge: Cambridge University Press, 1992.
Discusses the emergence of new forms of global governance in response to globalisation.

Dunn, John. *Democracy: The Unfinished Journey, 508 BC to AD 1993.* Oxford: Oxford University Press, 1992.
A collection of articles discussing the development of democracy in different parts of the world. As its title indicates, the book suggests that there is still a long way to go in making democracy more of a universal and satisfactory form of government.

Fukuyama, Francis. *The End of History and the Last Man.* London: Hamish Hamilton, 1992.
The author argues that we have reached the end of history, because there are no alternatives to capitalism and liberal democracy. Yet he raises the possibility that this new world will ultimately result in new discontents.

Held, David. *Models of Democracy*, 2nd edn. Cambridge: Polity Press, 1996.
A readable yet sophisticated discussion of different conceptions of democracy. The author concludes with a set of proposals for future democratic development.

Huntington, Samuel P. *The Third Wave: Democratization in the Late Twentieth Century*. Norman, OK: University of Oklahoma Press, 1991.
A discussion of the emergence of democratic institutions in countries that previously lacked democratic systems, casting a critical eye over some accounts of how and why this has happened.

Ostrom, Elinor. *Governing the Commons: the Evolution of Institutions for Collective Action*. Cambridge: Cambridge University Press, 1990.
A study of how appropriate forms of governments for common problems beyond the nation-state might be managed.

Paolini, Albert J., Anthony P. Jarvis and Christian Reus-Smit (eds). *Between Sovereignty and Global Governance: The United Nations, the State, and Civil Society*. London: Macmillan Press, 1998.
A set of discussions about the development of global governance following changes affecting the sovereignty of states.

Rosenau, James N. *Turbulence in World Politics: A Theory of Change and Continuity.* London: Harvester Wheatsheaf, 1990.

The author seeks to account for the persistent turmoil in world politics by evaluating the political, social and economic changes since the Second World War. He argues that we live in a 'bifurcated world' in which the old state-centric system is being challenged by a new multi-centric world of non-governmental organisations and collectivities.

Index